D. Ferris Arfaa hopes that the book will inspire others to take a journey through scripture to find, explore, and cherish the treasure chest of God's heart. Now retired in Delaware and an active participant in her church's Prayer Team and Bible study, this attorney-at-law turned poet graduated magna cum laude while earning a bachelor's degree in finance from the Notre Dame of Maryland University. A juris doctor degree followed from the University of Baltimore School of Law, as did many awards for legal and community involvement in Maryland. D. Ferris Arfaa was a Registered Nurse before receiving her degree in finance and an adjunct Professor of Business Law at the Notre Dame of Maryland University from 2000 to 2004.

Furthermore, this poet is the author of the collection of the eminently spiritual poetic verse first penned in 2006 in *The Gift of God's Word* (New Edition - 2023) and the motivational poems sparking a personal revival of faith in each of us released in 2021 in *From the First Nightingale to the Last: Poetry of the Salvation Song of Jesus Christ and the Twelve Apostles*. The release in 2023 of her current book, *The Gift of God's Heart* containing 41 spiritual poems realized from scripture and presented as a Biblical journey from Genesis to Revelation to find God's essence, represents D. Ferris Arfaa's continuation of the 'The Gift …' series.

For more information, please visit *www.dferrisarfaa.com*

I dedicate this book to the needs and desires of your heart in the hope that you should find in God's heart what you are seeking, while then, lovingly sharing what you find with others whom you meet.

"Put your hope in the Lord. Travel steadily along His path. He will honor you".

– Psalm 37:34

D. Ferris Arfaa

THE GIFT OF GOD'S HEART

AUSTIN MACAULEY PUBLISHERS™

LONDON * CAMBRIDGE * NEW YORK * SHARJAH

Ordering Information
Quantity sales: Special discounts are available on quantity purchases by corporations, associations, and others. For details, contact the publisher at the address below.

Publisher's Cataloging-in-Publication data
Arfaa, D. Ferris
The Gift of God's Heart

ISBN 9798889102502 (Paperback)
ISBN 9798889102519 (Hardback)
ISBN 9798889102526 (ePub e-book)

Library of Congress Control Number: 2023920991

www.austinmacauley.com/us

First Published 2024
Austin Macauley Publishers LLC
40 Wall Street, 33rd Floor, Suite 3302
New York, NY 10005
USA

mail-usa@austinmacauley.com
+1 (646) 5125767

With utmost, heartfelt gratitude, I acknowledge God's inspirational and motivational Holy Spirit for His guidance and strength though scripture to seek and find the treasure chest of God's Heart. He led me every step of the way.

Table of Contents

Author's Note

Have you ever planted a garden with the abundance of hope of creating a beautiful and blossoming landscape?

Have you ever gathered the seeds of the most prolific blossoms with the hope of future gardens that are equally as abundant and beautiful?

Have you ever pruned back a supposed flowering plant in the hope of restoration and renewal to salvage the garden that you created because it's beautiful blossoms never appeared or because they have failed to continue blooming as they should or because harsh weathering destroyed what you had begun? Did you, then, inspect each day after the pruning with great hope for any signs of new growth of fresh greenery, abundant new blooms, and grand restoration of original beauty?

Did you, then, water and provide nourishment in order to renew the weak, new growth, if any? Did you check every day for that hopeful new growth?

Did you protect the plant's fragility from further excessive heat, sunlight, battering winds, drought, or flooding rains?

If you didn't see fresh and new growth in the first few days, did you patiently and daily wait for any signs of recovery, renewed freshness and greenery, abundantly restored colorful flowers, or new shoots of fresh fruit? Did you check each new day with a hopeful heart that your failing plant that you love so much would show new, beautiful life that reflected your purpose for planting it and its purpose for living?

If you did any of the above things, you did so with a loving and caring heart. You did so with an unconditional love that seeks to bring new life to its creation that fell, for whatever reason, into purposelessness, ugliness, and death. And, friends, that's what God did throughout all creation's story. He patiently continues to do all those things for us when He corrects our faltering ways and woeful lives with the loving discipline of the hopeful, loving heart of a Father Creator.

The above checklist of 'have you ever(s)' is just a simple starting line for our journey into the search for our Creator God's heart. As a springboard, we all need to make our own heartfelt connection to a process of love with which we can easily identify. Let me tell you, friends, the above elementary garden experience is exactly the sequence of simple events that inspired me to seek and write about the extremely complicated and unconditional love that lives in God's magnanimous heart. In my faltering garden, I found and experienced my uncomplicated connection to our Father God's, our Creator's unconditional love that wants to make ALL things, no matter how battered, torn, or dead, new again with His loving care. Yes, dead, too! You read it right—'or dead'! So, I decided at that moment that no matter how much I loved and knew God, I did NOT really know Him nearly enough. I immediately felt that His PERFECT love for HIS creation amazingly exceeds all my limited love for my small, partially dead, withered garden in my yard where I spent many hours trying to create a beautiful space.

I, then, began a more profound search for God in God's Holy Bible. The verse found in Jeremiah 29: 13 jumped out and beckoned me to find God's heart by seeking it WITH my own. Our awesome and perfectly loving Father God gives us His promise through the prophet Jeremiah that when we seek HIS HEART WITH ALL OUR HEART, we will, indeed, find Him and know His heart, as well!

And you will seek Me and find Me, *when you* ***search for Me with all your heart.*** (Jeremiah 29: 13 NKJV).

In that one verse, He not only shows us the way, but God also promises that 'the way' leads to Him where He WILL be found by using our own hearts' seeking. To me, in that moment, He could not have made the path to knowing and experiencing the essence of His heart any clearer! It was God's perfect revelatory gift to me as He showed me the way. All we have to do, dear friends, is start the journey! All we have to do is wholeheartedly search for His gracious gift of heart!

Further, II Timothy 3: 16–17 tells us that we can be confident in our journey's enthusiastic search through His Word to His heart. It is 'God-inspired' or 'God-breathed'. It is the way. **We will, indeed, find Him when we seek Him there.**

All Scripture is given by inspiration of God, *and is profitable for doctrine, for reproof, for correction, for instruction in righteousness, that the man of*

God may be complete, thoroughly equipped for every good work. (II Timothy 3: 16–17 NKJV)

And so, I was ultimately inspired to write this book as a searching **trek through God's Word to find and know Him in the most intimate way— heart to heart!** My heart seeking His heart through His Word. His Word is our direct path to His heart's treasure. It is up to us to realize our personal connection by beginning the treasure hunt. As we traverse His Word, He will lead us directly to His treasure: His burning heart of unconditional love and 'life-giving', 'life-restoring' care; His sacred heart! We can't get lost if we stay on the path of His God-breathed Word. And, as we travel this journey, I want us to truly feel what God feels! I want us to deeply understand the awesomely perfect and sacred heart behind the feelings. I want our hearts to burn for Him as His does for us! And I want us to share the insightful, fulfilling journey together.

Let's start down our auspicious path and bask in the search's light for God's heart as one desirous group of faithful, tireless seekers. God's guiding light becomes brighter and hotter as we go. We can't lose our way if we stay dedicated to the end. We will sense utter excitement, peace, and astounding revelation on the way. It's our treasure hunt! And, surely, if we stay the course, we will find His treasure: His perfect and sacred heart! To that ultimate purpose, I offer this book of poetry, *The Gift of God's Heart, Poetry from God's Heart to Yours, as* the True North compass for our hunt. I hope you enjoy it as you travel with me through 41 spiritual poems, realized from scripture. If you complete our journey in 40 days and 40 nights, you will acknowledge God's immeasurable love for you (and you for Him) on the 41st day in my final poem, *How I Love You!*

Let's increase our hearts' passionate beatings together, as we communally pick up the pace of our hunt through scripture. God's heart will be our pacemaker. Surely, therefore, we cannot skip a beat, if we stay dedicated to the end! This poetic book, mapping the way to God's heart thrillingly stretches from my pounding heart to yours! Bon Voyage!

The Gift of GOD's Heart—Foreword

Author Dottie

Arfaa Foreword by Mark G. Magee

Oh the heart! Why should we give attention to the heart? The Old Testament prophet tells us, "**The heart is deceitful above all things and beyond cure. Who can understand it?**" (JEREMIAH 17: 9) Well, with man, this is impossible! But, with GOD all things are possible. In fact, the LORD GOD, our HEAVENLY FATHER wants to give each of us a new heart, a clean heart, a pure heart, a resurrected heart—HE wants to give us HIS HEART!

When I was a young child, I remember asking my dad, "Dad, since we live in the New Testament era, do I really need to read the Old Testament (After all, I really didn't like reading and the Old Testament section of my Bible was so thick!). I'll never forget his answer? "Mark, you really cannot understand the New Testament until you understand the Old Testament and you cannot understand the Old Testament until you understand the New Testament." And then he concluded, "Yes, we need to read and reflect and respond to both the Old Testament and the New Testament because it contains the HEART OF GOD!"

Our Heavenly Father has provided each of us many great and awesome gifts…Life, Love, Forgiveness, Hope, Joy, Peace, Meaning, Significance, a Relationship with HIM, and Family and so much more. But I consider HIS greatest gift to us to be is HIS REVELATION to us, HIS Holy Word—because it reveals HIS heart and thus changes ours.

That's why I am excited and thrilled to encourage you to read this book—**The Gift of GOD's Heart**. Our author, Dottie Arfaa, is a sister in Christ who loves the Word of GOD and understands that HIS Word is the means the LORD uses to transform our weary, weak and wicked hearts into a holy, healthy, whole heart just like HIS. I love how Dottie said it—This is just, "my heart seeking His heart through His Word."

My encouragement is that you use this book devotionally and reflectively one poem at a time. And use this book intentionally along with the Scriptures to pursue the Heart of GOD. I love the promise in JEREMIAH 29: 13…"**And you will seek Me and find Me, when you search for Me with all your heart.**" And not only will you find HIM, you will find a new, glorious, resurrected heart! My prayer for you is that your time in this book and in HIS Book, will assist you in Enjoying an Everyday Relationship with JESUS!

Enjoy and may the LORD GOD bless you with a renewed heart.

Mark G. Magee—Sr. Minister at THE CROSSING, Milton, Delaware.

Prologue

Truly know me and understand that I am the Lord Who
demonstrates unfailing love.
(Jeremiah 9: 24)

Do you know God? I mean, do you really KNOW God—not just know about Him or the things that He has done from random Bible stories or other books? Do you know the essence of Him down deep to the core of His heart? His thoughts? His deepest feelings? His longings? His joy? His heartbreak? His strength? His peace? His purity? His 'unfailing and unconditional love'? Have you pondered on Bible verses long enough to truly decipher the depths of the heart of God? That's an intriguing question, is it not? Luke 6: 45 reveals that our words are formed out of the abundance of our hearts. Thus, we, therefore, can expose the abundance of the truths of God's heart through His divinely inspired words in the Bible. Right?

So, do you know God's Heart? In Jeremiah 9: 24 above, He invites us into His heart. He invites us into His 'unfailing [heart] of love'! *The Books of Genesis* (written by Moses, 1410–1450 BC) and *Revelation* (written by the Apostle John, approximately 95 AD) in the Holy Bible give us the best insight into the heart of our Almighty God. It is there that we find God's heart of love, joy, peace, patience, kindness, goodness, righteousness, mercy, and compassion, faithfulness (i.e., the fruit of the Holy Spirit found in Galatians 5: 22–23), diligence, and judgment. Yes, judgment lives in His heart, as well. God is a fair, just, true, and mighty judge! Amen!

The Book of Exodus (also written by Moses, same time period as Genesis) shows us a commanding, guiding, watchful, and freeing heart of God in His demonstration of Almighty, Holy love for us, His children. As God leads the Israelites out of bondage from Egypt, He marks the path for them to freedom and the promise of a restored life in a secured, new home. He lovingly gives them His Holy Ten Commandments to follow in order to secure the best and safest path to that home. He is offering His faithful, steadfast heart as a guiding force to lead their way. Commanding, guiding, watchful, and freeing are the adjectives that I would use to describe the characteristics of God's heart found in *Exodus*. Possibly, you may find more.

We, also, can clearly see the essence of God's heart in John's Gospel, the *Synoptic Gospel of Matthew*, and the *Epistle of 1 John*.[1] *The Synoptic Gospel of Matthew*, along with the *Gospel and Epistles of John* richly tell us of where, when, and how our God Incarnate, Emmanuel (God with us), Jesus Christ, walked the earth and personally interacted on the closest, intimate level with us. They give us an astute look into who He was, is, and is to come. Matthew was an original Apostle who personally walked with Jesus. John was also an original Apostle who personally walked with Jesus, but additionally, held a special place as being particularly close to Him. You see, John, 'son of Zebedee', favorably occupied a place in Jesus' uppermost inner circle of four within the chosen Apostle group of 'Twelve Ordinary Men'.[2] Therefore, among the *Gospels and Epistles*, we will walk through Matthew and John because these two men experienced the greater, intimate relationship with Jesus Christ's heart. These books best demonstrate God's attempt to show us His sacred heart after we failed to understand and appreciate it from the time of creation onward to the incarnation, the Cross, and beyond.

Reverting to *Genesis*, I found and noted no less than fifty adjectives that describe the heart of God as follows:

---

[1] Karen H. Jobes (2020) *1, 2, & 3 John*, HarperCollins Christian Publishing, 501 Nelson Place, Nashville, TN 37214 USA. "Church tradition from the earliest days of Christianity has ascribed these letters to John, commonly believed to be the apostle John—one of Jesus' chosen twelve, the son of Zebedee, and 'the disciple whom Jesus loved' of John's gospel. But there's a problem. Neither the text of the gospel nor that of the letters bears John's name, or any name. Second and Third John are from the pen of 'the elder', who is not identified. The letters and gospel are anonymous to us, but the Christians who originally received them undoubtedly knew the identity of the author, and it is likely on the ancient testimony of those believers that the letters have been ascribed to John."

[2] D. Ferris Arfaa (2021) *From the First Nightingale to the Last: Poetry of the Salvation Song of Jesus Christ and the Twelve Apostles*, Austin Macauley Publishers LLC, 40 Wall Street, New York, NY 10005, noting Author John MacArthur, *Twelve Ordinary Men: How the Master shaped His Disciples for Greatness and What He Wants to Do with You (Thomas Nelson Books, Inc., Nashville, TN, 2002)*.

Giving	Relational
Creative	Sensitive
Energetic	Regenerate
Compassionate	Yearning
Loving	Purposeful
Pure	Kind
Merciful	Restorative
Forgiving	Redemptive
Humble	Tender
Understanding	Teaching
Sharing	Gracious
Fruitful	Good
Powerful	Yielding
Discerning	Guiding
Bonding	Longing
Hopeful	Prolific
Sacrificial	Productive
Patient	Introspective
Careful	Reflective
Thoughtful	Examining
Faithful	Fair
Enduring	Resolute
Selfless	Responsible
Sustaining	Judgmental
Unfailing	Lovely

Furthermore, reverting to *Revelation*, I found some of the same attributes as in *Genesis*. Of course, that's not unusual because we know that God never changes and is absolutely consistent in His character for all eternity. He is the Alpha and the Omega: the great 'I Am'. But, nevertheless, here I noted no less than thirty-three adjectives that describe God's heart. To prevent duplicity of the above list, I omitted traits that are redundant and noted only the additional qualities as follows:

Unwavering	Beckoning
Receptive	Gentle
Assuring	Passionate
Willful	Relentless
Diligent	Strong
Flawless	Perfect
True	Trustworthy
Joyous	Supreme
Whole	Royal
Searching	Attentive
Omniscient	Omnipresent
Omnipotent	Inviting
Seeking	Limitless
Everlasting	**Holy**

I'm sure that you may discover many more characteristics as you read the Bible. As you read the verses in the Appendices of this book, please pursue your own descriptions, as well. The bottom line fact is that we serve an auspiciously BIG and Almighty God with a magnificently HUGE and HOLY heart! A heart that was, is, and always will be Holy and perfect! A heart that beats with a life-giving capacity far beyond our most creative imaginations! Dear friends, He invites us to know Him! We, therefore, should want to seek, know, and understand God's heart, even if the journey for this divine treasure challenges our own human limitations. Agreed?

Jesus Christ was God Incarnate on earth (John 1: 14, "And the Word became flesh and dwelled among us, and we beheld His glory, the glory as of the only begotten of the Father, full of grace and truth"). Therefore, all of God's beautiful qualities found in *Genesis* and *Exodus*, apply to Jesus' perfect and Holy heart. *[For], all things were made through Him, and without Him nothing was made that was made. In Him was life, and the life was the light of men* (John 1: 3–4 NKJV). In the *Synoptic Gospel of Matthew* and the *Epistles and Gospel of John*, we learn about His perfect, loving, and holy heart in His relationships, His ways, choices, teachings, miracles, warnings, and admonitions. 'When we know God's heart, we know Jesus'. When we know Jesus' heart, we know God's. They are One and the same! God came to earth incarnate in Jesus, the Christ. He humbled Himself when He came to earth and put on our shoes. He took off the shoes of the heavenly King of Kings and put on the shoes of an earthly servant. He walked in our shoes so that He could demonstrate for all time that He beckons us, and He truly knows and unfailingly loves us. When His journey on earth was done and, as He looked forward to His ascension back to heaven, He said, "I am leaving you with a gift—peace of mind and heart." (John 14: 27). Here, God explicitly offers us ***The Gift of [His] Heart***.

Let's then begin finding God's gift of peace by seeking and knowing His heart. Remember the old saying, *You cannot understand someone until you've walked a mile in their shoes*? The author of that saying remains historically unknown, but it adeptly captures the principle that empathy or insightful understanding for someone else manifests from walking where and how they walked.

In this book of poetic verse, I attempt to place us in God's Biblical shoes: His shoes of creative and restorative humility; His shoes of hardship; His shoes of sacrifice; His shoes of purpose to the appointed end. And, along the way, through all else—His shoes of compassion, devotion, faithfulness, and love. Walk with God and Jesus throughout this book. Follow my poetic attempts to interject us into the shoes of God in the aforementioned Biblical accounts. Take a walk with Him and see mankind through His heart. As we imagine ourselves in His footsteps, we can better empathize with Him along with His feelings. We can, then, accept His invitation and further seek to know His heart. Our purpose on this journey is to ultimately know Him more intimately when we find the treasure of His sacred heart.

In the pre-Christian era, God's Biblical walks with us came during chosen, significant, and specific historical times. Attentively, He spoke, appeared, and revealed Himself as needed. During that time, 'when' God walked was informative of His character. But, upon walking with us as the Incarnate Jesus Christ, God always walked every day, all day, with all His divine character on display at every moment. For, we know that He was the same yesterday, today, and tomorrow (Hebrews 13: 8). He never changed and never changes! Therefore, after Christ, the adverb 'when' He walked is of no concern.

Hence, with Jesus Christ, true understanding and empathy for God's heart, can be derived if we place ourselves in His everlasting and faithful shoes following 'where' and 'how' He walked 'in the flesh'. Difficult to do, right? It's an uphill hike or search, for sure! And no uphill search or hike is easy. It will take time and energy. It will take concentrated study of the course. But the map of the course is charted by God Himself and can be trustingly followed to the desired finish line.

Let us, then, begin our energetic, uphill study with a walk in God's shoes. As we place ourselves in His shoes where He walked, we will gain immense insight into 'what' and 'how' His heart feels. We will feel what He feels now, how He felt 'in the beginning', and how He feels 'in the end' on into eternity. We will seek, experience, feel, and know Him better with a more deeply gratifying and finely-tuned insight into His nature. God's amazing gift of His heart will be found by us when we seek it with all our hearts. His heart is truly a treasure and it will be a magnificently valuable find that we can always cherish!

Before we go, though, it is important to understand and accept that a part of the uphill search will lead to avenues of deadly temptations that we can only overcome with Jesus' lead. Be ready for the evil surges to attack at various junctures. Their surge is not to immediately kill you, but, to lure you, through distraction, off the path to God's heart. At the end of the road of distraction, dwells a realm of deceptive evil leading to death. Now that you are aware of the dangers along the way, we can begin.

Come along. I hope you enjoy the poetic journey with me. Before each poem, I hope you will study the respective, true Biblical verses found in the Appendices. They are the stage for our visionary dramas along the respective allegorical poetic paths to discover God's heart. Walk through each poem as if you are on allegorical path in a treasure hunt. But remember, before you do, take your own shoes off and boldly place your feet in the footsteps of our Almighty God. Step deep into His shoes and feel, as best we humanly and imaginatively can, where and how He passionately walked throughout time. Along the way, open your minds to alternative ways of loving and living life's journey. I hope that together, we gain an insatiable desire to continue to know God better as we gain true feelings for His loving heart on our own devoted and allegorical journeys.

Jesus says, *Arise and let us go from here*…(John 14: 31). So, your shoes off—on your mark, get set, ready—let's go!

Chapter I
God's Creative, Relational, Hopeful, and Restorative Heart

(*Genesis* 1–6: Verses in Appendix A)

We can see, experience, and feel God's creative, good, purposeful, hopeful, patient, kind, caring, longing, sharing, fruitful, relational, judgmental, and merciful, heart of exemplary love in the *Book of Genesis*. A lot of adjectives describe His Heart in this Biblical account, for sure! In fact, as we look through *Genesis*, we can find every defining characteristic in our foregoing list. I'm sure you will find more, as well. *Genesis* 1–6 walk us through God's creation story. It is 'the beginning' of our walk with Him. For your review, the respective Biblical accounts are found in Appendix A.

After reviewing Appendix A, join me in a poetic, allegorical vision and symbolic design of our own imaginative landscape and garden according to God's creation steps. We will feel His magnanimous hope, joy, love, and sense of accomplishment as we walk in His shoes. We will feel His immense dismay and disappointment when He has to cast judgment on His creation's evil doings; but also, we will experience the endless depth of His merciful love when He displays His healing and restorative measures for posterity, lest we die.

Poem: *Imagination Heart* (Genesis 1: 1–31; 2: 1–4)

In my imagination, my home's landscape carefully planned I on day one
picturing every type of plant, flower, color, hue, shade, and source of the sun
I knew there must be light for my creation to thrive and to grow strong and true
The light, the plan, the care must be perfect, to perfect all the plans that I drew

And lovingly, imagined I with great hope for lasting beauty to flourish,
lasting design and beauty that, through hopeful love, would I tenderly nourish!

In my imagination, my home's landscape carefully planned I on day two
How wondrously gorgeous my hopeful plan would evolve based on all that I knew
I made room between each plant to separate each in its own lovely fine space,
giving respect to the integrity of the elements of each one's place

And lovingly, imagined I with great hope for lasting beauty to flourish,
lasting design and beauty that, through hopeful love, would I tenderly nourish!

In my imagination, my home's landscape carefully planned I on day three
The soil must be rich, give nourishment with just the right load of water be
For each plant and flower must reproduce others of their same inclination
They should be seed-bearing plants to keep growing restored, renewed population

And lovingly, imagined I with great hope for lasting beauty to flourish,
lasting design and beauty that, through hopeful love, would I tenderly nourish!

In my imagination, my home's landscape carefully planned I on day four
Just how much light needed to shine, what kind of, when, and if there needed be more
or less with darkness of night's cooler shadows to give reprieve from the day's heat
Just the right light is needed by day and just the right darkness needed repeat

And lovingly, imagined I with great hope for lasting beauty to flourish

Lasting design and beauty that, through hopeful love, would I tenderly nourish!

In my imagination, my home's landscape carefully planned I on day five
plants and flowers for butterflies, bees, other insects to adorn and thrive;
colors and berries planned I that hummingbirds, other birds, and dragonflies love;
plants, flowers, birds, insects, and more needed in my landscape to hover above

And lovingly, imagined I with great hope for lasting beauty to flourish,
lasting design and beauty that, through hopeful love, would I tenderly nourish!

In my imagination, my home's landscape carefully planned I on day six
walkways, benches, tables, chairs, sunshades for family, neighbors, friends—
a great mix
More types of trees in the landscape's yard, planted I for every creature's use
Oh, what joy seeing the beauty of my landscape's creation alive—profuse!

And lovingly, imagined I with great hope for lasting beauty to flourish,
lasting design and beauty that, through hopeful love, would I tenderly nourish!

My imagination's landscape filled with life's breath; my joy soared on day seven
Looked I with amazement, beholding such beauty comparable to heaven
Rested did I in my satisfied excellence of my landscape's completion
This day could I rest because with love I gave life to my landscapes' creation

And lovingly, imagined I with great hope for lasting beauty to flourish,
lasting design and beauty that, through hopeful love, would I tenderly nourish!

With great joy gazed I on my awesomely beautiful and adorned space to bless
"It is good, it is excellent," thought I as I enjoyed my plan's fruitfulness
The fruits of my labor, thought I, would be heavenly for all time's duration
Keep growing and producing well for all the inhabitants' procreation

And lovingly, imagined I with great hope for lasting beauty to flourish,
lasting design and beauty that, through hopeful love, would I tenderly nourish!

Poem: *Heavenly Pursuit* (Genesis 2: 7–19; 2: 20–25)

With the fullest love, pursued I, to keep my landscape special and everlasting
An attendant, required I, to enjoy my creation's space while basking
in the morning's eastern glow, feeling the intensity of sun's vital light,
while looking forward to the peaceful beauty of the bright stars and moon by night

I envisioned an eastern garden in my landscape where lush plants could take root
Then, with a sustainer's care, I caused water's flow to every eye-dazzling shoot
and out unto the rest of the landscape, I made the blue, clean refreshment flow
out to the four corners of my original design, sustenance to show

I brought my attendant and informed him in all aspects of my garden's care
I showed him of which plants, flowers, trees, and fruit to consume in my garden there
As I was watching my attendant nourish and groom my colorful, green place
Noticed I, a partner for him was required for completion of this space

The attendant and partner met in my eastern garden, the first time to see
They joined together for the tasks at hand and equally yoked to thrive and be
Neither was now alone; and excellent matched company they happily kept
each other in all times of abundant living, knowing love's joyous concept.

A throne seat, placed I, for my attendants to rest and take in the garden's sights
They could spend time enjoying ALL the garden's images colorful delights
For I knew that we ALL need relaxation during work to keep us 'til night
A place to sit, rest, reflect, think, correspond—make relationships sound and
tight!

My thoughts stayed profusely consumed with the marvelous garden's colors
and sight
And lovingly, imagined I, in revelry of lasting beauty's delight
I bonded with enduring love as I on passion's perch mused the whole night
through,
as pleasing visions of my attendants, plants, flowers, good fruits, and creatures
grew
Patience would I need to behold the fullest of my imaginative view!

And lovingly, imagined I with great calm for lasting beauty to flourish,
lasting design and beauty that, through hopeful love, would THEY tenderly
nourish!

Poem: *Commiseration Touch* (Genesis 3: 1–24)

My musings of My landscape and garden permeated ALL My nights and days
Each moment of reflection upon its beauty and care brought fresh life that stays
The attendants enjoyed overwhelming peacefulness at their coveted work
I was aghast to discover that betrayal in My garden, neath lurk!

The rules for attending My sweet garden were supposedly clear from the start:
weed and mulch the beds, prune the plants, pinch back the flowers—enjoy fullness of heart
And be careful for snakes that neath the plants may lie and wait in despise unknown
They will strike and bite to cast you out from your lovely place, near the garden's throne

Not heeding my words, the attendant's partner reached into the shrubbery lush
Bit by a snake, her hand was torched by venom and her face greatly burned a flush
My attendant checked on his partner where she lay; bit, as well, he quickly fell
Now, both compromised there place by disregard for my warnings to heed, full well

They surely knew that their bare apprehensions were horribly, openly shone
I understood, though, that they could not yet comprehend their problems, yet unknown
I went to offer My help, but they were frightened with knowing their condition
Their trouble was clear—obviously they had disobeyed My admonition!

Because of their profound disobedience: out of My garden, I them cast
Never to return to the sweet, easy work of the lush garden of their past
Out they must go to the unkept landscape to work harder than ever before
They now would feel in painful labor what the rest of the landscape had in store

I chased the snake and made sure that he in my garden could never a man bite
without sure retribution from the stricken man's quick, strong, and deadly
blow's smite
My attendants would suffer the lack of the freshness and wealth of My garden
Now, to the outside soil they must return, as the sun's heat does dry and harden

Before leaving My garden, My sorely overwhelmed attendants, did I give
refreshments and clothes for their trek made from My own hands for their hard
life to live
I placed formidable gates on My garden's openings and known ingresses
Never again could they return to the garden's life, which sealed nature blesses

Poem: *Everlasting Hope* (Genesis 4: 1–15, 25–26; 6: 5–8, 11–13)

I visited My former attendants in their home of hardship enduring:
Two sons now blessed them and a family strongly stood, hopefully securing
a future together that God may see, show pleasure, and kind restoration

After all, thought the man, God joined us forever in our interrelation
Upon seeing Me, their two sons brought gifts for My welcoming's fullest favor
Delighted was I appreciating their kind, thoughtful gifts, I would savor
One son's gift showed lavish thanks for My hoped for, but unexpected, appearance
The other son's gift was insulting, without recompense for past wrongs clearance

I broken-heartedly rejected the insulting gift so that son would learn
the importance of respect and concern for others, his selfish heart did spurn
I desired the selfish son to know righteousness for his soul to be saved
Intended I, the rejection to show him a road to new life, not yet paved

I wanted him to live according to God's rules of relationships and thrive
I wanted him to learn the ways of respect and love—be profusely alive!
I wanted him to have the best, and the vast fullness of life for him to know
I wanted him to experience everything good by first goodness to show

My lesson fell upon the dead heart of that son in just one day of sad fate
He turned a good day into tragedy by killing his brother with great hate
Jealousy and a sinful nature guided him to his most wretched demise
becoming a fugitive from justice, cast out from favor to realize

But I sent an order out to all four directions of my surly landscape
'Touch not a hair on this son's head or seven times the crime befall your vile nape'
So, a mark on him, I placed to give notice to those who want to wreak vengeance
'Touch him not, he need live his life in an appropriate and due repentance'

When My former attendants requested my blessing on a new child to bring
I gave My blessing and restored life upon them by stunningly offering
more acreage in My landscape for the new son to inhabit and procreate
new generations of life that through Me would they honor and impregnate

In My imagination, thought I that good things would spring forth pure and survive
the snake's venomous bite, the hateful son's murderous plight: even love may thrive
And hopefully, imagined I with great calm for lasting love to now flourish,
lasting love and justice that, through hopeful life, would THEY tenderly now nourish!

But My hopes for their good lives lay trampled as evil stomped across landscape's ground
No purity remained; no time shown unstained by evil's maleficent sound
The love, justice, and goodness of life that I imagined for them to flourish
lay dead forever never to thrive, never to tenderly, gently nourish.

So, all must be destroyed, declared I, as I pondered time's wicked corruption

I must wipe out My first landscape's caress with a great flood of vast destruction

No life should be spared, save one shown good with his offspring to stand strong and survive

In my imagination, new hope sprung forth for their loving spirits to thrive

And hopefully, imagined I with great calm for lasting love to then flourish, lasting love and justice that, through hopeful life, would THEY tenderly now nourish!

The Deluge (Francis Danby 1840)

Chapter II
God's Steadfast, Guiding Providential Heart

(*Exodus* 16; 20; 23: Verses in Appendix B)

As we walk through the *Book of Exodus*, Chapters 16, 20, 23, in Appendix B, we find that Almighty God is just that—Almighty in all things of a Holy Father. He is an all-powerful wondrous and magnanimous provider of our daily needs, the founder of our disciplinary requirements for living a holy life, a compass for our earthly journey through each day and night, an all-knowing and wise ruler over all creation, a completely caring and loving Father attempting to focus our lives and goals for our goodness and the goodness of others, and a devoted, steadfast watchman with a loving interest in guiding our steps through life. It's our responsibility to understand the depth of His love so that we can follow His lead and hold fast to His principles. Let's try to stay close to His steps as we continue our journey together to find His Heart!

Poem: *Freedom Walk* (Exodus 16; 20; 23)

As a I looked at My child take her first steps in wonder of how far she had come
I knew she would need guidance through all life's challenges, not just her chosen some
With a guiding presence, as all good parents do, I stood steadfastly ready
to offer My hand in support should she now not be strong, upright, or steady

My child's way, I carefully checked for any flaws so not to stumble or fall,
so not to sway from the path that I nurtured with love and My heart's beating call,
so, to keep her moving straightforward, growing balance, confidence, and great strength:
amid all the choices of direction, as the walk increased in yonder length

My child must rest, refresh, and eat as the way would grow frightfully strenuous
A place to lie down with greenery abound, fresh bread and meat—continuous
Complete freedom was My ultimate goal in the culmination of her days
She must be well-taught and provided-for to prevent endless burdensome ways

As My child expanded her stride, the need for tighter rules fell upon life's ground
She must honor and obey Me for greater freedom to be skillfully found
That was My first command in order to release her to a vicious vast world
For her welfare and goodness, I penned rules for her life—with love, mindfully burled

The rules—there were only Ten for now that would suffice to maintain her mapped way
The first, she received in an honor code for respect to her Parent to stay
I laid them out simply in a plain format for My child to read and comply
All had strictly pure, deep, and clear meaning with no correct, true path to belie

My pen wrote: Work hard all week long, but give the week a deserved final day's rest;
Do no harm to any person, stay pure, and steal not for your days to be blessed;
Manage your life with integrity, no false witness strikes on your soul's accord;
Take from your own labor alone, covet not your neighbor's sought and fine reward

As I penned these rules, My hopeful heart leaped with abundance of satisfaction
Now, My child could go forth knowing well the way to step, seeking true correction
Surely, My child will not stray, My heart hoped, as I made her path perfectly clear
Surely, she would follow My lead, keep her way, and to My heart ever grow near

My Ten Commands were sufficient at the start of My child's stepping out from Me
I would monitor her steps in life for to discern if different ones need be
My child would always be My child and never far from My heart's great affection
Though she be far from home, My heart's beating pulse resonates her home's direction

My child's way, I carefully monitored to offer help upon a stark fall,
So, to continue the path that I nurtured with love and My heart's pounding call,
So, to keep her moving straightforward, with new balance, confidence, and grand strength
amid all the choices of direction as the walk increased with yonder length

My child would always be My child and never far from My heart's great affection
Though she be far from home, My heart's pounding pulse resonates her home's direction
Complete freedom was My ultimate goal in the culmination of her days
She must be well-taught and provided-for to prevent endless burdensome ways

My child would always be My child and never far from My heart's free-spending love

Though, so far from home, she'd be near in My heart, eternally beating above

My child would always be My child and never far from My heart's great affection.

Though she be far from home, My heart's pounding pulse resonates her home's direction

GUIDANCE TO FREEDOM

Chapter III
God's Transcendental, Purposeful, Humble Heart

(*The Synoptic Gospel Of Matthew*: Verses Found in Appendix C)

Throughout Matthew's Gospel, Jesus Christ is magnified as the Holy Son of God, the Messiah. Although he tells of many episodes regarding his walk with Christ, Matthew makes Jesus' identity as the Son of God his main theme. From the beginning, Matthew tells of Jesus' holy birth, which was the incarnation of God through His Holy Spirit. He then continues emphasizing His holiness throughout His life to the end at the sacrificial Cross.[3]

In Matthew's Gospel, therefore, we will continue our search for God's loving heart within the scope of Jesus' deity on earth as 'the Son of God': His divine birth, His humble and tested beginnings, His blessed teachings, His holy miracles, His sacrificial and saving death, telling and restorative resurrection, and essential ascension into heaven back to God the Father, so that He could share eternity with us.[4] Remember, ***God gave His only begotten Son*** (John 3: 16) are the first six keywords we want to look at in order to see His extremely bountiful, loving heart.

As we pursue this journey together, let's feel what God and His Son, Jesus Christ, feel. Let's try to sense His (the Two in One) holy emotions on every level. Imagine yourself with His love, longings, disappointments, or joy. Feel His communion with you as you understand Him more profoundly. Examine His feelings through the humble gift of His Son. With every step leading up to

---

[3] Pastor Reagan, Jimmy R., (January 14, 2013) The Reagan Review, 'The Theme of the Gospel of Matthew.'

[4] *Id.*

Christ's birth, imagine yourself in the place of the Father Creator and probe your feelings about His fervent heart. Try to feel what God felt as He looked at His defiant creation, but then, gave us His only begotten Son.

After the birth of Christ, change your hiking shoes and shift your imagination's gears to be a follower of Jesus as your newly discovered Master (teacher), Immanuel, Shepherd, and Messiah. As we go, you will surely feel a sense of immense closeness to both hearts: the loving, giving, fervently almighty heart of God as our Heavenly Father; and the purposeful, obedient, passionate, bleeding heart of Jesus as God Incarnate, our Master, Shepherd, and Messiah. So, let's go! Let's now follow Him, Jesus, the Christ…

Poem: *Sanctuary Road* (Matthew 1: 18, 20–23; 2: 23; 3: 1–3, 17)

I rule the most peaceful place in My restful sanctuary
No wayward soul or unknown troll dwell there, in caring wary
Boundaries lay between Me and they who live within the pen
of restless souls and wayward trolls, the place of defiant men

The pen sears a diametric space at the heart of My peace
Within the pen, some souls cry out for My nurturing release
But the boundaries are high from them to My reservation
How can I break the walls, I thought, and change their destination?

My heart mourned at the pen I created that now shows no peace
How could I go to them within and give nurturing release?
They cannot see Me, cannot feel Me, or know My heart's pure call,
unless I transcend to them in there, by breaking through the wall

To transcend, I thought, would not be hard, nor difficult to do
I would change Myself to be like them for all their dreams come true
So, in I went placing Myself within the womb of Mary
She is pure and good, I thought, and will trust My soul to carry

Must I appear in the best, mean, or worst habitat therein?
Is it best for Me to live with them who painfully know sin?

I must shame Myself beyond the birth to live where wealth is none,
to know the least, create a feast for communing with the Son
I will call My name 'Immanuel': God with them, as the One

Nazareth, I chose, as My debut to commune with the men
who were the lost ones, sifted and tossed, by human nature's sin
I must be true to My Prophets who faithfully spoke My Word
revealing to the lost that, first, in Nazareth I'll be heard

And I must announce the purpose of My coming to their land
John the Baptist should pronounce, "Repent—the Kingdom is at hand;
Prepare the way of the Lord, make His pathway straight [and clear]";
Come to Him with open hearts and minds to feel His heart beat near

In I went as One with them and lived within their seared, penned space
My love so vast, My heart beat fast to transform them through My grace
You see, not only had I produced their space within the wall,
I created every one of them by virtue of My call

First, I went to John, baptizing at Galilee's Jordan flow
He must baptize Me in river's stream for righteousness to show
My Body rose from baptismal stream, My Dove came from above,
landed upon My head, shimmering pure holiness and love

My love so vast, My heart beat fast to transform them through My grace
My love so great, My heart felt joy to transcend among their space
So, those who choose could now live in a new-found, redeemed fashion
My heart leaped with joy as I previewed their saved lives with passion

Nothing meant more to Me than to secure their future blessings
No other place but one with Me, to grace them with My dressings
My love so vast, My heart beat fast to transform them through My grace
My love so great, My heart burned fire to transcend among their space

Those who choose can now come home, I'll lead them each step of the way:
step by step to My sanctuary where peacefully they'll stay
I rule the most peaceful place in My restful sanctuary
The wayward souls can now come home upon My arms to carry!

Know the Dream Come True

Poem: *The Holy Way* (Matthew 3: 13–17; 4: 1–4)

The Holy way is straight and narrow, no hidden maps for our surprise
Follow the road that bright Jesus leads from sunrise to each new sunrise
Humble yourself with a gentle heart, begin the road like Christ's story:
baptism at first to cleanse your thoughts and lead to showing God's glory

God's glory always reveals God's heart, as heaven glows God's guiding light
by opening its door, flooding us with God's Holy Spirit in sight
As Jesus was baptized, God spoke, "This is My Son, My beloved [One],"
led by My Spirit as your shining guide for My straight path to forerun

Surely, those who watched did wonder in awe at divinity's bright glow
How could they see such astonishing wonders and of Me not to know?
'This is My beloved Son'—strong words resounded with the bright white dove

'I Am well pleased with Him'—a striking voice boomed from the sky above
You must follow in His gracious, bold steps to bear My burning love
Surely, those who have missed a child, must wonder at Divinity's Gift
of God's One begotten Son into their paths and for their lives uplift
How great the blessing of this Gift for all the world to know and cherish:
a sacred offering to them to seek His way, so not to perish

In seeking His second birth: first Mary, and next through Holy Spirit—
find, through Him, the straight and narrow way, for our souls to Him secure it
But, the way is long, though narrow, with challenges along the marked path
There will be times in a wilderness walk, God's strengthening heart, must hath

The devil will come to tempt you and take you from your led and straight way
Hunger and fatigue will entice you to accept temptation to stray
Face the devil's pitch with Jesus' strength as He rebuked temptation
Stay on the bright and marked path, and give no heed to dark inclination

Follow the path that Jesus forged, when tempted by the sly, crazed devil
You shall succeed by the hand of God—devil's buttressed voice to level
And, when you've refused the temptation of things by the devil's sly hand
You're on your way to the abundance of life that God's way doth command.

Seek God's way with all your heart's passion and you'll find what you're looking for
Remember the long path is straight and narrow, but leads to God's blessed door
It's when you see the clearing before you, as you forge the wilderness
that clear vision of where your life must go, your mind and heart now possess

Now we can walk in the guiding light to reveal God in His glory
Heaven will glow with a bright white light illuminating His story
God's glory always reveals God's heart as heaven glows God's guiding light
by opening its door, flooding us with God's Holy Spirit in sight!

Praise God from Whom all blessings flow from His holy way!

That Through Him the World Might Be Saved

Poem: *Do You See Him Walking?* (Matthew 4: 13–17, 18–25; 9: 35–38)

Our trek has been long and hard; our path has been narrow, but, grandly clear
Do you see Him now? Over there! Look fast! He calls for them to be near
He's calling for Peter and Andrew at the sea's edge of Galilee
After leaving Nazareth, He came to Zebulun and Naphtali

It's Jesus, the bright light of our new way and true path to the treasure
of our hearts' beating realignment, pounding each beat for His pleasure!

How enjoyable His warmth and His gracious, peaceful voice echoing
He shouts to the workers to follow His path, by His light's beckoning

Dark was our journey as each mapped way fell to the wilderness' night
Deep were the fearful valleys causing worry, hopelessness, death, and plight
But now, we can see Jesus, Who is showing us the Father's bright glow
through the fire in His heart for us, the Father to follow and know

We are getting closer and can almost hear His heart's welcomed pounding
We have waited long on our journey to see His image resounding
a definite way before our eyes that we should find by His True North
Now we have found Him! See! His bright fiery heart beats the path set forth!

Now, see Him calling two men known as James and John, sons of Zebedee
They, like Peter and Andrew, dropped everything to follow and see
the new path that we, too, are taking with the teacher from Galilee
No longer shall we fear not seeing our way clear from plight to be free

Quickly, gain your footing close to the One Who is leading the True Way,
so, our hearts will beat for Him and with the Father at the end to stay
See! He is teaching, preaching, and clearing the path's huge bumps and deep
holes
See! His way prevents fatigue's illness and presents lessons to unfold

Quickly, more are joining our group as we journey all day and night long
We want to be near Him, feel His heart's flushed beating, passionately strong
We want to be close to His sure footing, feel the warmth beneath His feet
We want to remain close to His teachings for our journey to complete

But wait, stand back now! Infected souls approach Him to be healed and
blessed
Chilling be their afflictions: leprosy, diseases, demon-possessed
Watch! Healing He brings to all who seek the heat of His heart and new life
So, let's restore our nearness to His heart's fire, not fearing such strife

Jesus is fearless and bold with a heart for the deathly sick and lost
He beckons them come for the healing and new life, no matter the cost
If we follow Him, we, too, can learn the path to serve others, as well:
to serve, living fearlessly with His bold example to show and tell

Galilee, Jerusalem, Judea, and Jordon River to see
underneath our feet, so, in keeping with Him, steadfast our posture be
We want to be close to His sure footing, feel the warmth beneath His feet
We want to remain close to His footsteps for our journey to complete
In every step behind Jesus Christ, we feel His Sacred Heart beat!

Poem: *The Compassionate Coming* (Matthew 4: 23–25; 9: 35–38)

See, they are coming! Do you see them amid the dawn's first hues?
They have heard of the **Master's** coming; they have heard the good news!
Miracles preside in His coming as He heals ALL of them,
from Galilee, the ten towns, Judea, and Jerusalem

He's also teaching with parables and a woe-filled saying
that touch the depths of our hearts to prevent humanly straying
So, let's sit and listen as our **Shepherd** bids us to come rest,
by drawing us near with His staff, from His pure Words to be blessed

Come, sit, listen, hear of our blessed **Master's** vast journey's travels
Know what He has done, where He has gone…what ills He's unraveled
The **Master Shepherd** telling parables so as to relate
valuable lessons of this life to change our deserved fate

By His tales of life and His rejuvenated parables
He grows our hearts, rests our weary lives with thoughtful potables
Relationships He values as He calls our faithful heart's stay
Come, sit, listen, hear, receive the beloved **Savior's** mastered way

Come, sit, listen, hear of our blessed **Savior's** vast journey's travels
Know what He has done, where He has gone…what ills He's unraveled

You will feel loves compassion for the goodness of all God's seed
He continues coming from God's garden, gracing each one's need—
First **Master**, then **Shepherd**, then **Savior**: coming to share His Creed!
Come blessed **Savior**, come!

****

It's important to understand that God is a relational person. After the fall of mankind into evil and before the saving grace of Jesus Christ, God had to live completely separated from us by barriers. Only His high priests could enter the Holy of Holy spaces for limited and set times. God's desire, however, throughout time has been to dwell with us and have a personal relationship with each of us. Now, after Jesus came and died for us, He can live in us through His Holy Spirit. He can be with us on a personal level.

God desires to give us His heart, no matter the cost! When Jesus healed the masses, He tirelessly gave us His heart. We cannot even imagine the unlimited degree of illnesses Jesus met in the large crowds who followed Him. We cannot even imagine the repulsive appearance of the wounds and diseases that He faced with a loving, smiling, and compassionate look. "Oh, to feel and have God's heart!" should be our plea. My poem below, *All His Heart*, attempts to capture all His heartfelt love for all of us, for all time. The question remains, "Can we follow in His shoes with all His heart for all others?" Or when the going gets rough and temptations are great, will we stop and turn back to our old ways? How is your heart?

A Rhetorical Poem: *All His Heart* (Matthew 1–28)

Oh Lord, tell me!

How was His heart when Jerusalem expelled Him from our midst?
Was His heart broken, was He oppressed and crushed, was He eclipsed?
Was His heart still glowing with the light of holy magnitude?
Was He overflowing with holy love, faithful to exude?

Oh Lord, tell me!
How was His heart when from Pharisees' temple He was cast down?

Was His heart shattered with sorrow or adorned with God's heart's crown?
Was His heart peaceful, loving, resolved to His blessed called work?
Was He staring back with God's love, enduring each evil smirk?

Oh Lord, tell me!

How was His heart when to the sick masses He chose to depart?
Was He resolute to His task, was He faithful from the start?
Was He bidding farewell to ALL as from them He turned to go?
Was He focused on His task to healing of the masses show?

Oh Lord, tell me!

How was His heart when multitudes sought His powerful, stored touch?
Was He withholding His powerful love, not to wield much?
Or was His heart tenderly caring and giving ALL He could
to heal ALL with His holy power as we know that He would?

Oh Lord, tell me!

How was His heart as His true love, the masses loudly pursued?
Was He offering Himself freely for ALL lives be renewed?
Was He holding each close to His heart so no parting render?
Did He pursue the wayward with His heart gracious and tender?

Oh Lord, tell me!

How was His heart as every sin was dropped at His holy feet?
Was He courageous, victorious over ALL to defeat?
Was He strong against colds, fever, palsy, leprosy, madness?
Did He meet ALL sickening sights with no moments of sadness?
Oh Lord, tell me!

How was His heart as He healed ALL the sick masses who followed?
Was He filled with hope as He removed them from where they wallowed?
Was He glowing as He changed lives and saw ALL futures brighter?

Was His heart's love amplified as our ailments became lighter?

Oh Lord, tell me!

How was His heart as He appeared to His beloved believers?
Was His heart open to heal them ALL, though some be deceivers?
Was He fervent with His healing touch, as their ill lives He spurned?
Could we ALL watch as He worked, so from pure love and His heart learn?

Oh Lord, tell me!

How was His heart when many doubted Him with hearts of hatred?
Was He forbearing of their sins, revealing all things sacred?
Was He dressed in heartfelt goodness, compassion, and devotion?
Could we see Him and learn His ways—for others be His potion?

Oh Lord, tell me!

How are our hearts as we witness His heart's warm and healing fire?
Are our heart's healed from His passion to inflame His heart's desire?
Are we healed and changed, stoked with the fire of His molten heart?
Are we loving, kind, comforting in our ways from each day's start?

Oh Lord, tell me!

How are our hearts when many doubt us with sin's heart of hatred?
Are we forbearing of their sins, revealing all things sacred?
Are we dressed in heartfelt goodness, compassion, and devotion?
Have we learned to spread His heart's ways as a life-healing potion?

Oh Lord, tell me!

How was His heart?
Yes, You are well-pleased!
Oh Lord, tell me!
How are our hearts?

How is Your Heart?

In His teachings through parables, Jesus was showing God's relational, loving, and compassionate heart by demonstratively presenting how others experienced, successfully endured, and overcame similar burdens that we now may face. What a wonderful way for Him to show that He truly cares!

From my poem, *Of Miracles, Parable, and Woes*, in *The Gift of God's Word* (2006, where you can also find Jesus' specific parables in poetic verse) please enjoy the following poetic verses of Jesus' ministerial journey, surely evidenced by Matthew as he explains in Matthew 4, but, found detailed in scripture in Luke 7–20:

Poem: *Of Miracles, Parables, and Woes*

Jesus walked through the land and with His Apostles resided
Then, with words and pure hands touching, His miracles presided:
He healed the sick, raised the dead, and gave sight and hearing,
preached to the poor and all sinners, in grand humility appearing

He asked that they spread not the word of His healing
for he knew of the Pharisees and the ways of their dealing
He knew that God's work remained to be done
to complete Isaiah's prophecy of God's chosen One

But the word of His wonders spread as fast as lightening
Masses sought Him out; to them nothing was frightening
but to be without Him or His promise of healing
They cared not who knew Him or with whom He was dealing

When John the Baptist in prison heard of the same,
John sent out his disciples to ask Him His name
Jesus sent them back to John to report what they see:
that much healing takes place of the lame, the blind, of leprosy...

After John's disciples left, Jesus spoke to the crowd:
"John's the messenger, the preparer," He proclaimed aloud,
"John's the greatest of men who were born on this earth;
he's the Elijah, the preparer of your soul's rebirth"

"If you have ears to hear, you must hear of John's way
that was made for you to be saved and with God stay
But, if you hear not, repent not, then, woe to you all
for your lives will crumble, your cities will fall"

Jesus went out to more cities in preaching with travel:
anointing, forgiving, offering parables to unravel
He spoke in parables to make His lessons command
to ones though they heard, they may not understand

So, of His parables, we will speak not at all in retort,
but, in sublime submission to their divine report
of the seed's sower, the bright lamp, the Samaritan good,
the rich fool, the fig tree bearing not as it should

Of the mustard seed, the yeast, and the narrow door,
of the great banquet, the lost sheep, the lost coin, and more,
of the lost son, the shrewd manager, the widow's persistence,
of the Pharisees and tax collector, the rich ruler's existence

Of the ten minas to servants increased by all but one,
of the tenants at the vineyard and the owner's son,
of the coming of God's Kingdom, of those left shaken,
of Lot's wife leaving Sodom, of those saved who are taken

He taught 'The Lord's Prayer', the 'Six Woes' to resent
He taught watchfulness, no worry, and encouragement
He taught of sin, faith and duty, of Jonah's first sign
He taught the last shall be first and the first in last shall resign

Now, speak of the 'Six Woes' of which we should carefully listen:
the first says, "woe," love God and let justice glisten;
the next says, "woe," take the humble seat in the den;
the next says, "woe," repent, do well—and be known by all men;

The fourth says, "woe," make the laws fair and supportive;
the next says, "woe," or be blamed for all life abortive
the sixth says, "woe," by your practice of wisdom teach:
if you practice what you teach, you reach whom you preach

In His parables, Jesus spoke to the unschooled to hear
so that all men might know Him and to God's ways be near
His parables were given from His merciful, pure heart
Next, hear them again, deafen not, and from ignorance depart!

So, of His parables, we will speak not at all in retort,
but, in sublime submission to their divine report
of the seed's sower, the bright lamp, the Samaritan good,
the rich fool, the fig tree bearing not as it should
Of the mustard seed, the yeast, and the narrow door,
of the great banquet, the lost sheep, the lost coin, and more,
of the lost son, the shrewd manager, the widow's persistence,
of the Pharisees and tax collector, the rich ruler's existence

Of the ten minas to servants increased by all but one,
of the tenants at the vineyard and the owner's son,
of the coming of God's Kingdom, of those left shaken,
of Lot's wife leaving Sodom, of those saved who are taken

If you have ears to hear, God's Word you must heed!
Such was given for your saving in the form of His Creed
A Creed that when followed will support each and all
so that our lives will not crumble and our cities won't fall

Poem: *Come Sit Upon the Rock*

We've followed Him thus far, inspired by seeing
His Masterly teaching and ways of His healing
Now His Shepherd's heart calls us to sit and draw near
In His presence: the Rock and the Savior appear!

Come, sit upon the Rock for your life to be blessed
Come, sit upon the Rock from weariness to rest
The **Master** is speaking, the wind whispers, "rejoice!"
It pleads you to listen to sweet tunes of His voice
Come, sit upon the Rock for your life to be blessed
Come, sit upon the Rock from weariness to rest
The **Shepherd** is leading, the scene beckons to stay
He gives you refreshment to continue the way

Come, sit upon the Rock for your life to be blessed
Come, sit upon the Rock from weariness to rest
The **Savior's** heart is burning with warmth for your night
It bellows flames of His love for our hearts' delight

Come, sit upon the **Rock** for your life to be blessed
Come, sit upon the Rock from weariness to rest
From the summit of the mount, Beatitudes flow,
rushing like rivers from His heart for you to know

Come, sit upon the Rock for your life to be blessed!

COME, SIT UPON THE ROCK

From my poem, *The Beatitudes* in *The Gift of God's Word (2006),* please review once again Jesus' teachings on life in *His Sermon on the Mount.* His teachings as our Master directly lead as our Shepherd to His passionate, pure heart as our Savior who desires to help us find and live a righteous life. Come, sit, briefly place your walking shoes aside, rest from the journey, and listen with all your heart to the outpourings of His.

Poem: *The Beatitudes* (Matthew 5–6–7)

First temptation, then preaching, then the disciples call,
and the healing of the sick with miracles not small;
Then, the crowds fell upon Him and great lessons ensued
to teach His disciples the Beatitudes

'Blessed are those who are poor, mourn, and meek;
Blessed are those who righteousness seek;
Blessed are those who show mercy and heart;
Blessed are those who seek peace and from evil depart

Be the saltiest salt and the brightest shining light
and throw down not yourself to herein worldly spite
Put your lamp on the stand and give light to all men
Shine your light everywhere, shine again and again

Jesus changed not the law but fulfilled its rewards
to expand the scope of our expectation toward
each man to another by his practice and deeds
so, the law would improve this life and our needs

To say "do not murder" is not enough to cope:
we must judge not each other to fulfill God's scope;
we must love each other, anything less, we falter;
settle adversity first, then pray at God's alter

To say "adultery commit not" in the bodily flesh,
Fills not God's scope of our lust's sinful mesh
with adultery, which we commit with a lustful heart:
it's the same transgression, so from all sin depart!

Man is married 'til death, so in life "divorce not"
the spouse you have joined in creation's plot
to give birth to true union through faith and conviction,
a holy, pure state with lasting love and depiction

Praise be the Lord, swear not an oath to His name
Simply say "yes" or "no": such proclamation's the same
as the purest of answers, which need not a sworn word:
a sworn oath of your word stems from evil procured

No tooth for a tooth, nor an eye for an eye,
no revenge for the evil of days gone by
Simply turn your cheek to an assault's first touch;
go one more mile from the first, give the requester much

Love your enemies and pray for those who cause pain
On the righteous and unrighteous, God sends upon rain
Only loving who loves you, gives no reward to the soul
Be as perfect as God, our Lord, to extol!

Give to the needy, but not to be honored by men
Announce not your gifts, secretly wield your pen,
aiding others through gifts unseen and unknown
Not known by others, before God you are shown

Offer your prayer in secret to our Lord, as well
Choose few words, don't babble in a pagan swell
Simply state "The Lord's Prayer", "[God's] will be done"
God knows your needs with each rising sun

When you fast, look not somber as hypocrites do
Wash your face, on your head place an oily dew
Show freshness when for the Lord you are fasting
Fast in secret and, in secret, His rewards will be lasting

Store not earthly treasures that become destroyed
The love of money is the root from which all evil's deployed
Store up your treasures in God's everlasting realm
where your heart joins His with all good at the helm

Therefore, do not worry about life's eat or drink,
about your clothes or your house, you must not think
for God knows your needs and will to you give
all things, if you seek first His Kingdom to live

Judgment for judgment and measure for measure,
You will get in return for what judgment you pleasure
against all others who you judge for their actions
Judge not, be not judged for your personal infractions

Ask for the answer and seek for the finding,
knock for the opening, all knowledge unwinding
to those who ask, seek, and knock at God's door
We stand rich in the asking, thus in wisdom not poor

Do unto others as you want done unto you
No greater law of God can we each now pursue
for this law sums up all the law and the prophets
It's the Golden Rule by which all life profits

Enter God's realm where only some can pass through:
the narrow gate finds life gained by scarcely a few
for wide is the gate that leads to destruction,
where many pass through losing life's construction

You should know your acquaintance, do not be asleep
Many bad wolves are disguised as harmless good sheep
So, look to their fruit and you will know what you should:
good trees can't give bad fruit and bad trees can't give good

For Me to know you—it takes more than, "Pray Lord":
you must do God's Will with a powerful fiord!
Obeying God's Will means more than miracles casting,
if you want me to know you in the life everlasting

Therefore, hear these My words and employ their stock
They're your way to true life with a house built on rock
where it's foundation is strong and built for a lashing,
resisting a storm—homes built on sand come down crashing'

The Beatitudes are God's laws and direction for life
Follow their path to be free from every day's strife
for God knows His creation with all its contention
Beatitudes shows us the way to His Holy dimension!

Sermon On The Mount Of Beatitudes Poem

Poem: *He Cares* (Matthew 14: 6–33; 15: 32–38)

Friends, at our journey's start, we knew not what God had in store
We felt unsure, lost, empty, hungry, scared, wearily sore
Now, we know the pure Truth that our beloved Jesus revealed
In His Sermon on the Mount, He leaves no wisdom concealed

The Sermon on the Mount or the Mount of Beatitudes
Named 'Beatitudes for lessons to which Jesus alludes
in His preaching to us to make our journey less taxing
The Caspian Sea Mount, lush green and blue for relaxing

Sermon on the Mount—completed, but surely not over
The Shepherd revives our journey in sweet fields of clover
His name is **Jesus**; He lives the pure Truth, thwarting concerns
Our **Master**, our **Shepherd**, our **Savior**: for whom our heart yearns

Yes, our heart yearns for the Living Truth that sweet Jesus brings
His heart yearns more for our saving through the song that He sings
The blessed song of the Master, Shepherd, and Savior King
opens our hearts to His pure love so we, too, can His love bring

Compassionately, Jesus cannot betray His own heart
He began our trek with love and with love He will depart
But see! He calls come and eat, there is sustenance for all
Don't worry what you eat or drink, 'come now—eat, is My call'

Living Word of Truth, He resisted sending us away
He built a feast from small provisions—requested our stay
and broke bread and fish for all, while in doubt we looked upon
His miracle of giving on the anchor we sat on

Doubt vanquished as Jesus fed five-thousand: with just two fish
and five loaves of bread; His heartfelt love filled every dish
A wonderment begat before our very grateful eyes!
Fear not! The journey's remainder, He equally supplies!

Oh my! Pray, tell me why Jesus left the mount's holy feast?
Apostles came, spoke in His ear; He's disturbed, at the least!
His cousin, John, met his end because Herod claimed his head
John the Baptist in prison killed: Jesus' loved one dead

Living Word of Truth: He cares more than we now envision
Time will tell as we know Him well from His blessed provision
Worry not when His absence from sight claims our secure guard
He will return; He left for prayer in yonder garden yard

Surely, He mourns, but Jesus prays through His undeserved grief
He retreats to His solitude for welcoming relief
Surely, He will return to lead us, His flock, and resume
the journey's blessed offerings, which from His love we consume

His heart faithfully calls to us: 'Always be of good cheer!
In every tempest of every storm, I'm steadfastly near!
Do not doubt for I will catch you, if you succumb to fears
Just keep your eyes fixed on Me as My saving hand appears.'

Friends, at our journey's start, we knew not what God had in store
We felt unsure, lost, empty, hungry, scared, wearily sore
Now, we know the pure Truth that our beloved **Master** shares
He lovingly gives all for us, He shows that True Love cares!

He is our fearless **Shepherd** Who secures for us the path
He rescues us from every storm of ills from nature's wrath
He endows us with blessings each step of journey's way
He seeks us to remain with Him—so, not our hearts to stray

Let us stay the True course with Him until the journey's end
Surely, He is the **Son of God,** Who wants our ways to mend
Now, we know the real Truth that our blessed pure **Savior** holds
He wondrously cares for our needs as His heart to us unfolds

Blessed be His holy name, **Jesus the Christ, Son of God!**
He truly cares!

He Cares

Poem: *The Love of Little* (Matthew 18: 1–7)

Our trek is commencing as the disciples bend His ear
Come, let's listen, draw closer; far from His wisdom, I fear
Jesus speaks of loving the little ones first, above all
He speaks of humility that grows honor out of small

He speaks that honoring a child is honoring so Him
He speaks only as a child, we to heaven enter in
He speaks do no harm to the little ones: His loved best
He warns harm not the little ones or wrath's at His behest

He loves the little ones and the humility they hold
He loves the little ones; warns of punishment to unfold
for all who cause a little one to stray or lose her way,
you are lost from His presence with no mercy on display
Now, as we walk, let's speak of Him for He, too, began small
A sweet babe in a manger: arrived humble above all
Life's eternal treasure: wrapped first insignificantly
Behold Him as He was, as He is, and as He will be

God Almighty, how small You were when coming to our earth
But a babe in a manger, swaddled in love at Your birth
You came as You went, dressed in love made from cloth linen white
Little Child, Son of God, small but Holy, at love's first sight

Your love of little apparent when You came, when you stayed
You always loved the little ones; for their goodness, you prayed
And, telling of Your Kingdom warned all must childlike become,
humble themselves like children or apart from Him succumb

You spoke that honoring a child is honoring so Him
You spoke only as a child, we to heaven enter in
You came as You went dressed in love made from cloth linen white
Little Child, Son of God, humble but Holy, bright, white, Light

THE LOVE OF LITTLE

Poem: *The Bethany Table* (Mathew 26: 1–13)

In Bethany, we, with Jesus, a loving home have entered
Simon the Leper of the house, abides here, Jesus-centered
For, healed was he by our blessed Savior's powerful, sweet hand
Now, ALL are free to rest within for with Jesus, we do stand

The Bethany Table is set openly for supplying
the needs of wayward lives, weary hearts: upon hope relying
See the food that Simon prepared for His Healer's refreshment
Jesus invites us to dine with Him, without cost from us spent

We ALL are welcome to sit with Him and feel His blessed power
Does His time with us end too soon, He speaks of His final hour?
Comes one with expensive oil to anoint His holy head
Surely, she feels that terribly nigh, our Savior's death, we'll dread

She seems intensely aware that the full of oil must be spilled
upon the head of Jesus for His life's burden be fulfilled
Grumbling fills the air as Apostles jeer her kindhearted deed:
'Too much was spilled, too great our cost, of it we have greater need!'

With His loving ways and kindly heart, Jesus simply replied:
'She honored Me with her generous deed, it shall not be denied!
The woman's giving heart in the whole world shall be heard and known
She seeks My sweet aroma with her deed of sacrifice shown

Soon, I will not be with you, but your called ministry will last
Move beyond your ill will for her; feel her passion as it's cast
Give your love to her now, as to you My lasting love I give
You will sense My sweet aroma as I die for you to live

You will spread the Gospel when I'm gone for all the world to hear
See that when of her you speak, you share her memory held dear
For she seeks to savor Me now and revere My life's presence
She knows the value of My heart and seeks its holy essence
Savor Me and My time, as well, as the woman now has done
Be tender to ALL childlike souls who draw nearer to the Son
Give your love to her now, as to you My lasting love I give
You will sense My sweet aroma as I die for you to live!'

Poem: *The Return* (Matthew 21: 1–11; 23: 37–39)

Jesus walks before us, onward to Jerusalem to stay
Mentions nothing of His weariness, though long has been the way
Four days we have followed from Galilee's lush, green, and blue shore
Four days Jesus led us; four days with us, He traversed before

Into Jerusalem again appears His destination!
Mount of Olives beneath our feet, comes His new proclamation:
'Fetch that good donkey and her colt on Bethphages' yonder yard;
Tell her owner that, "I Am" here that he may release his guard'

Entering we must; entering we do: from the gate transcend
to make Jerusalem His final place on our journey's end
Steadfast, He forged the way beyond the gate of God's blessed city
As if purpose to disclose from journey's long complicity

'King of Kings, Hosanna in the Highest,' roars the gathered crowd:
cheerfully and tearfully shouting their grand praises aloud
The stomping of the donkey's feet upon the fresh, bright, green palms
Such music revives our weary ears as Christ lays down His alms

What must He be thinking on this bright, beautiful, new found day
The Journey's length nearly at its end; memories to replay
His mind on our way's togetherness, the strength from Him became
our passage to the fullness of His heart, which our hearts proclaim

The Crown of His Kingdom must surely be fixed before His eyes
We venture onwards to His goal to bring freedom for our lives
King of Kings, Hosanna in the Highest: the donkey, His throne,
as He passes His Kingdom's people with purpose all His Own
Focused in purpose, resolute to His teaching journey's end
Healing still as He passes before us, hope and love to send
Focused in love and healing, how blessed our new way shall become
We feel relief at journey's conquest for sure this is **The One**!

Jerusalem cried out, 'Who is this brilliant healer and friend?
Why has He come? Where is He from? Is it for our lives to mend?'
He is: 'Jesus, Son of David, messenger from Galilee!
He came to raise up His Kingdom before our closed eyes to see!'

Hear His beckoning voice as He calls us to His humble throne:
'I AM here and have come to make you all My tendered, blessed Own
Come live with Me now, My Heart offers you My Kingdom's safe sword
to fight your earthly battles; I come in the Name of the Lord!'

King of Kings, Hosanna in the Highest: the donkey, His throne,
as He passes His Kingdom's people with purpose all His Own
Focused in purpose, resolute to His teaching journey's end
Healing still as He passes before us, hope and love to send

'King of Kings, Hosanna in the Highest,' roars the gathered crowd,
cheerfully and tearfully shouting their grand praises aloud
and bowing down before Him, adorning His feet their fresh palms
Such sights and sounds revive our spent souls, as Christ lays down His alms

Hear His beckoning voice as He calls us to His humble throne:
'I AM here and have come to make you all My tendered, blessed Own
The Crown of His Kingdom must surely be fixed before His eyes
We venture onwards to His goal to bring freedom for our lives
Come live with Him now, His Heart offers you His Kingdom's safe sword
to fight your earthly battles; He comes in the Name of the Lord!'

'Blessed is He Who comes in the Name of the Lord!'

THE RETURN

Fellow seekers, this is a great time for us to pause and rest. We are near are journey's end. It seems that Jesus wants personal time with His closest followers because I see them walking up the hill to the orchard. Apparently, Jesus is taking His Apostles for a special session upon the Mount of Olives. Be patient, waiting for them to reappear. Surely, they will share His message with us. In the meantime, let us remember and relish Psalms 107 together for it sums up all that Jesus has done for us on this long journey to Jerusalem. In verses 1–9, it says:

Oh, give thanks to the LORD, for He is good! For His mercy endures forever. Let the redeemed of the LORD say so, Whom He has redeemed from the hand of the enemy, And gathered out of the lands, From the east and from the west, From the north and from the south. They wandered in the wilderness in a desolate way; They found no city to dwell in. Hungry and thirsty, Their soul fainted in them. Then they cried out to the LORD in their trouble, And He delivered them out of their distresses. And He led them forth by the right way, That they might go to a city for a dwelling place. Oh, that men would give thanks to the LORD for His goodness, And for His wonderful works to the children of men! For He satisfies the longing soul, and fills the hungry soul with goodness. (Psalms 107: 1–9 NKJV)

Truly give thanks to the Lord! The disciples share Jesus' message with us in their ***Olivet Awakening***: *The Olivet Discourse* (Appendix C). Praise the Holy One!

Poem: *The Olivet Awakening* (Matthew 24: 3–44: The Olivet Discourse)

Jerusalem, Jerusalem, sweet Olivet waits mention
Gathering His disciples, our Shepherd sits for attention
They gather close to the Holy One, lean near on bended knee
He rarely sits calling forth His ranks; our closed eyes hence to see

How rare His love, His concern, His great heart for us more to know
He's speaking now of things yet not here, of things to come now show
Why tell of future's comings, not yet arrived, and sound so grave?
He warns, it seems, to make for us a forthcoming life to save!
First and last, in generalities that unknown lives will feel

But take heed, He speaks also of Daniel's prophecy to seal
Our generation, He says, will know of Jerusalem's fall
He warns what actions we should take to live beyond city's wall

Jesus proclaims, 'Do not fear, though frightful things must come to pass:
famines, pestilences, earthquakes, wars, persecution—alas!
You must survive to the end, for your life be ransomed by Me
Be strong, remain in My love, one day My glory all will see!

You are My elect, for My elect My promises shall stand
to rescue you from tribulation's evil powers at hand
My love remains strong through all earth's wrongs, right to the very end
Stay close to My love, hold to My heart: for this life to transcend

My warnings stem from My heart's flaming love, passion, and concern
Take My heart's love to your heart, be wise, strong, take heed and discern
between what is wrong or right, and how the future to survive
Until the end, this life transcend: with Me, remain alive!

For I must leave, but will return at the ending of the Age
in clouds on high with angels nigh to call out your new life's page
Of that day or time, I cannot tell, for no one knows the hour;
The season shows as the fig tree grows buds before the flower

Watch for that day of My return as winter returns to spring
Keep your eyes fixed on Me while of My return faithfully sing
I love you, Am coming for you; spread My love throughout the land
All will hear, more coming near; Hallelujah, My love will stand!'

How rare His love, His concern, His great heart for us more to know
He's speaking now of things yet not here, of things to come now show
Why tell of future's comings, not yet arrived, and sound so grave?
He warns, it seems, to make for us a forthcoming life to save!

Jerusalem, Jerusalem, sings the Savior's Olivet
Throw yourself upon His heart's fire and with His love beget

to all the world His burning love, in His passion so remain
Hallelujah, hallelujah, hallelujah! With God reign!

Poem: *The New Day* (Matthew 27: 1–2, 11–14, 27–31, 39–44, 50–54)

We welcome the new day, the new dawn, the new fresh vision
that fills us as we, with Him, complete His holy mission
Our expectations stand high as our Sheppard passes by
brightly lighting up our path in the peaceful morning sky

This new, bright day surely brings new hope for each tomorrow
as Jesus walks and talks, healing each one's long-held sorrow
He has shown His steadfast love to ALL right from our wayward start
He cared not from where we came; just offered His tender heart

The Master Who brought us together, now soldiers have snatched:
the result of Pharisees' plot from silver ransom hatched
Horror fills my soul, as I look upon the gruesome sight
that takes our Master far from us, while He puts up NO fight

To the Governor Pontius Pilate, Jesus now appeared
He offered Himself no defense, as crowds upon Him sneered
'You say you are the King of Jews,' is that not rightly so?'
'It is as you say,' Jesus said, 'for in your heart you know'

From Pilate's tent, they led Him out before soldiers to mock:
A crown of thorns, a handheld reed, a scarlet robe for smock
Spat upon, jeered upon, taunted with, 'Hail, King of the Jews'
He endured all the day's pain for the rapture of Good News!

They hung Him on a Cross for blasphemers to see and say,
'You who are the Son of God, save yourself upon this day!'
Ridiculed as one who IS sin by elders, chief priests, and scribes:
all drunk on hypocrisy that each sinful heart imbibes

When end had neared and all was spent, His cost we cannot know
With all He suffered on that Cross, love only He did show
He cried out to God, 'My Father forgive this day their deeds!
They know not what they do and know not how to nail their needs!'

As His voice called, 'It is finished,' He gave up His Spirit
The veil was torn, the earth quaked, graves opened that were near it
The Centurion and his guard, who watched our Savior die,
feared God and said, 'This was God's Son'; the saving Cross stands nigh!

We welcome the new day, the new dawn, the new fresh vision
that fills us as we, with Him, complete His holy mission
Our saving grace stands high as our blessed Savior hangs aloft
bravely lifting up our lives as we mourn and grieve His cost

We welcome the new day, the new dawn, the new fresh vision
that fills us as we, with Him, complete His holy mission
His saving grace held on high as beneath we kneel and say,
'This is a new vision, a new fresh dawn, a new fresh day!'

This new, fresh day surely brings new hope for each tomorrow
as Jesus suffered on the Cross, healing each one's sorrow
He has shown His steadfast love to ALL right from our wayward start:
lifted up on the Cross, sacrificed all to give His heart

Spat upon, jeered upon, taunted with, 'Hail, King of the Jews'
He endured all the day's pain for the rapture of Good News!
Hear the Good News: Jesus, our Savior, paid the total cost

So, ALL be saved to the new day and none be claimed as lost!
Blessed be this new day!
Truly, Jesus is the Son of God!
Hallelujah to the King of Kings!

Interlude

Before we follow John's *Gospel and Epistle* on the continued path to seek and find God's Sacred Heart, I, firstly, want to share my poem, *Wondrous Love*, which was inspired by a devotional written by Charles Spurgeon derived from Psalm 17: 7—*The wonders of Your great love.*[5]

I feel that this is the appropriate place to present it, and rest together in His astounding, sacrificial love before we follow the Apostle John to Jesus' Heart because John spoke of himself as, 'the one that Jesus loves' (John 13: 23). And it was John to whom Jesus, upon the cross, gave His mother for safekeeping as He told His mother that John was now her son, and, told John that Mary was now his mother (John 19: 26–27).

The wonders of His unimaginably great love must never escape us!

VERSES

(Psalm 17: 7; John 3: 16; 13: 23; 19: 26–27)

Show Your marvelous lovingkindness by Your right hand, O You, Who save those who trust in You from those who rise up against them.

Psalms 17: 7 NKJV

For God so loved the world, that he gave his only begotten Son, that whosoever believes in Him should not perish, but have everlasting life.
JOHN 3: 16 NKJV

---

[5] Spurgeon, Charles (1995) Morning & Evening, A Devotional Classic for Daily Encouragement, p.282, Hendrickson Publishers, Marketing, LLC, Peabody, MA.

Now there was leaning on Jesus' bosom one of His disciples, whom Jesus loved.

John 13: 23 NKJV

When Jesus therefore saw His mother, and the disciple whom He loved standing by, He said to His mother, Woman, behold your son! Then He said to the disciple, Behold your mother! And from that hour that disciple took her to his own home.

John 19: 26–27 NKJV

Poem: *Wondrous Love* (Psalm 17: 7)

The world is filled with wonders, but the apex of the Cross presides
overwhelmingly above them all, where His heart alone resides
With alms, we give our hearts to Him never reaching with full blown sail
to repay Him, measure for measure, His cost paid to tear the veil

Now we can sail with Him to shores beyond, despite our wanting alms
He paid our cost upon the Cross, forfeiting favors to our palms
The favor to be one with Him, He placed beneath His gestured feet
Calling us to partake of His grace, when OUR sins He did defeat

How warm His heart giving us FULLY what alone He should possess,
placing in our hands the keys to pure life—share in His holiness
I can't imagine the fire that burns in such a heart as this
I only hope that from this day, my life redeemed, I dare not miss!

He bids me, 'come,' to dine with Him, even though death will find Him there
He says that He will bring the food, so in His giving we can share
His bread and wine of life, partaking of blessings He gives for all
New life has come, new hope abounds, redemption reclaims our fall

We placed Him there upon the Cross, exposed to North, South, East, and West
No one has ever felt before THAT fire burning in His chest!

I could see the glow of His love-spilled heart, when His last breath did fail
His Spirit's wind fanned His blazing heart with a gracious, stunning gale

The alms He left upon the Cross as He forgave us with His lips
mercifully save us, while from His sacrificial cup He sips
How could this be? He purely forgives when the blame is ours to bear!
For WE shamefully sinned, causing HIS pain, agony, and despair!

In His mercy and love, He rejoices though painfully aloft
Though beaten, scorned, broken, shattered, and torn, His heart still richly soft
The scent of spikenard fills the air, which only His heart could produce
His heart's affliction spills sweet aromas for guilty souls seduce

Come one, come all to receive His love at His beckoning crossed feet
calling us to partake of His grace, as OUR sin He did defeat
How warm His heart giving us FULLY what alone He should possess;
placing in our hands the keys to His heart, sharing His holiness

The world is filled with wonders, but the apex of the Cross presides
overwhelmingly above them all, where His heart alone resides
With alms, we give our hearts to Him never reaching with full blown sail
to repay Him for His sacrifice and cost paid to tear the veil!

His Wondrous Love

Chapter IV
God's Holy Sacrificial Heart

(*The Gospel of John*: Verses Found in Appendix D)

For God so loved the world that He gave His only begotten Son, *that whoever believes in Him should not perish but have everlasting life. For God did not send His Son into the world to condemn the world, but that the world through Him might be saved.* (John 3: 16–17 NKJV)

The keywords leading us to God's heart in John 3: 16 are **'God so loved,' 'He gave,' 'His only begotten son,'** and **'so that the world through Him might be saved.'**

And, in 1 John 3: 1, we see that God loves us, His creation, so much that He calls us 'His children.' Here, the keywords in our search for God's heart lead us to the pathway of understanding that God speaks of **His depth of love as our Father Who calls us 'His children.'** He, therefore, is our Father God! He is our Creator parent! He is our Father and Creator God Who humbly gave us Himself in Jesus Christ, God Incarnate, to be sacrificed for us, so that we might be saved!

Behold what manner of love the Father *has bestowed on us, that we should be called **the children.*** (I John 3: 1 NKJV)

Any good and loving parent knows that he or she would give her last drop of blood for the life, safety, and welfare of her children—even though on many occasions, we feel that they don't deserve it. In fact, without a second thought, we would give our very hearts, the pump of our life's blood! But, even if we are good and loving, we as humans are not perfect like our Father God in heaven by any means. We as imperfect, but loving, earthly parents would give everything to save our child, no matter how deserving or not. We should never forget, dear ones, that our Father in heaven is just that—our heavenly Father and Creator, 'Father God,' Who is perfect in every way and cannot be less! So, how much of His perfect love and heart would He give to save us?

As a perfect parent, God, cannot love us, His children of His creation, in less than a perfect way. The word 'perfect' means 'without fault or defect, flawless, satisfying all requirements.'[6] He did, in truth, give His last drop of blood on this earth in exchange for our lives, both physical and spiritual, through His sacrifice of His first born, only begotten Son, Jesus Christ, on salvation's Cross at Calvary. He came to earth and humbly gave Himself to us. He gave us His incarnate heart at Calvary and nailed it to the Cross! Make no mistake, He gave it and He nailed it! We, the humans in the event, are just the instruments of His sacrificial purpose to show us His love. We are undeserving beneficiaries of love's perfect, unconditional, and sacrificial gift of God's heart! How can we expect less from Him, our perfect heavenly Father, than what we imperfectly give to our own underserving children? Surely, we do not!

But parent or not, you can feel why God gave and poured out His life's blood through Jesus Christ for the saving of our lost lives for all eternity. As we witnessed on our journey, He had tried before to save creation's story with love's hopeful heart through the great flood, Noah's heirs, and an exodus of the Jews out of bondage in Egypt to a promised land of pure, sweet, fruitful living. He hoped that would cleanse and restore His creation of all our evil inclinations. We know that didn't last. We know God's heartfelt efforts fell short of His mark.

Thus, out of His ultimate demonstration of His perfect love, He came forth with His last resort effort to bring about needed change in our depravity. He humbly came to earth as Jesus Christ to show us how to live and then, find the way to His perfect love. He came as one with us. He lived as one with us. He taught as one with us. He endured all temptations that inflict us. He suffered all afflictions as one with us. And He died a criminal's death in our places as a sacrifice on redemption's Cross for our sinful ways. As the perfect, loving parent, He took the ultimate punishment that we deserved. He stood condemned for us. He 'satisfied all requirements' in order to give us His perfect heart and show us the way to redemption and salvation. But, as if that weren't fully enough, He did not stop at the grave to show us the way. He arose from the dead, left the tomb empty, and gave us a way to eternal life with Him.

---

[6] Merrimack-Webster Dictionary

His loving, passionately flaming heart, with all the goodness it offers, is overwhelming to say the least! We should all fall on our knees in awe at the very thought of that kind of perfect love.

Retrospectively, look again at our walk through *Genesis* and *Exodus* to reflect upon what had transpired beforehand in our relationship with God. We had strayed extremely far from Him and His original and perfect plan for our lives. We were not heeding His guidance and prophetic warnings. We were at the brink of eternal self-destruction with our inhumane behavior to others. We were not listening to His Word. We were stubbornly disobedient to His commandments. We had failed to grow His shown love, patience, kindness, goodness, peacefulness, faithfulness, mercy, compassion, obedience, and truth in our hearts. We were 'utterly helpless [in our depravity]…and, it was the right time…[to show us His true, perfect, and ultimate love through Jesus Christ's death on the Cross. It was the right time to restore us to a wonderful, new relationship with Him].'[7] Finally, in complete and perfect truth through sacrificial love of His only Son in our places, He gave us His perfect heart! He gave us Himself!

At Jesus' resurrection, He broke the chains of death for believers forever; and, upon Jesus' ascension to heaven, He gave His heart's Holy Spirit (His essence) to indwell with us forever. We see the culmination and meaning of the legacy of God's heart when Jesus told us before He ascended to heaven and departed:

Those who accept my commandments and obey them are the ones who love me. And because *they love me, my Father will love them. And I will love them and reveal myself to each of them…All who love me will do what I say. My Father will love them, and we will come and make our home with each of them.* (John 14: 21–23)

****

---

[7] Romans 5: 6–8, "When we were utterly helpless, Christ came at just the right time and died for us sinners.

But God showed his great love for us by sending Christ to die for us while we were still sinners. And since we have been made right in God's sight by the blood of Christ, he will certainly save us from God's condemnation. For since our friendship with God was restored by the death of his Son while we were still his enemies, we will certainly be saved through the life of his Son. So now we can rejoice in our wonderful new relationship with God because our Lord Jesus Christ has made us friends of God."

We've been on the road to God's heart a long time. We have endured the journey right to the gates of Jerusalem upon Jesus' final return from Galilee. The road to finding the fullness of God's heart is shorter now, but it gets bumpier and more challenging from here. The Apostle John, however, who is 'the disciple who Jesus loved' (John 21: 7), will clear away the threats and bumps as we listen to his message of love and delight in Jesus' road of sustenance and salvation. We will lose all fear as we will now be able to accept that we can rejoice in the journey's suffering through Christ's love for us at the Cross. We can expect to hear John point out all the landmarks that show Jesus as our Creator of all things, everlasting Almighty God, our Heavenly Father Who provides where He guides (Isaiah 58: 11[8]), our loving Messiah, Lord, and Savior. The finale of our travel will lead to the sacrificial Cross and beyond, but, when we understand and receive all the magnificent blessings through to the journey's end, we will be glad we came, resisted the temptation to leave among other 'dead ends' along the way, and stayed the course! We will rejoice!

Now that we are refreshed and prepared, let's continue to go with John…

Poem: *Starlight Struck Judea* (John 1: 1–5, 14, 16–18; 3: 16–21; 8: 12)

Starlight struck Judea and 'The Light of the World' was born
We did not know at the time that upon His life we'd mourn,
that He, only for us, His impoverished life would give
the riches of His Kingdom and eternal life to live

He is the Beginning and the pure Word from heaven sent
Son of God, Incarnate One, Creator for our lives spent
His light too bright, His truth too right for this world to cherish
Given freely from God's heart, so none on earth would perish
Flesh God became and, in the flesh, willingly for us paced

---

[8] Isaiah 58: 11, "The Lord will guide you continually, And satisfy your soul in drought, And strengthen your bones; You shall be like a watered garden, And like a spring of water, whose waters do not fail."

Dwelled among us—a crocheted cover: grace and truth so laced
upon our lives that we could bear to behold His bright light
and see the fullness of His love not blinded by the sight

Flesh, God became as Jesus Christ, so all the world be saved
Flesh, God became as Jesus Christ, so roads of life be paved
When we receive His light, showing the road's new saving way
We will never wonder from His sight, welcoming our stay

Raised upon the Sacred Cross of Life, God's flesh met death there
His loving heart defeated death and raised us from despair
Now, we who believe in new life at His feet mutely Crossed
Behold His pure sacrifice and to winds our sins be tossed

'For God so loved the world that He gave His only [pure] Son'
to save all who would believe and receive Him as The One
Light of the World, He vaporized darkness with His bright glow
Giving eternal life to all who toward His light would go

Starlight struck Judea and 'The Light of the World' was born
We did not know at the time that upon His life we'd mourn,
that He, only for us, His impoverished life would give
the riches of His Kingdom and eternal life to live

Poem: *Everlasting Bread* (John 6: 26–40)

Bread of life! How shall we seek and find it on this vast way?
God should supply it as when with the Israelites did stay
in the desert with Moses and no fresh bread to be found:
manna from Heaven to eat, gently placed upon parched ground

Jesus spoke:
'Look to Me and My ways to ascend life's eternal stair
"I AM" the Bread of Life everlasting, sealed by God's flare
Come to Me, follow Me, believe that God sent Me to give
life's bread everlasting so that all believers may live

For it is the will of our Father that none should perish
Come to Me now, for eternal life's fullness to cherish
God sent Me for this—to save all, who eat of His great love
and seek My bread's stairway for life to ascend by His Dove

Come to Me now; I will lose none who follow Me to find
the greatest kind of love ever known on earth to mankind
Come with Me now, be lifted up on creation's last day
God's Will be done, 'I AM' eternal life, the Truth, the Way

"I AM" the True Bread of Life, God's Gift stored under His care
My supply never runs out and great abundance lulls there
Everlasting life preserved by the love of the Father
for all who take and eat, then at His table would gather

Look to Me and My ways to ascend life's eternal stair
"I AM" the Bread of Life everlasting sealed by God's flare
Come to Me, follow Me, believe that God sent Me to give
life's bread everlasting, so that all believers may live'

Poem: *The Heart of God's Home* (John 13: 1–7; 14: 21–23; 15: 11–17)

God's Heart dwells among us, He longs for our hearts: no sin
The Heart of His home knocks our door, pounding to come in
With every lasting beat, His Heart pounds passion's pure love
Louder and louder it pounds, pelting our hearts whereof

God's Heart kneels before us, He humbly shows us His way
Bowing down to wash our feet, His vast love on display
His Heart shows gentility with its final heart's sound:
'Love one another as I love you; make love abound'

Jesus commands us live as His chosen blessed loved fruit,
loving each other with His pounding heart's pursuit
Pound on one another's hearts, like God pounds on our door
Louder and louder still, until your hearts beat no more

Jesus is leaving us soon; He tells us to believe
His joy remains in us, so our joy from Him retrieve;
No greater love than His as His life for friends He gives;
'I choose you, give your life as one for the other lives'

God's Heart shows humility with its final heart's sound:
'Love one another as I love you; make love abound'
No greater love than His as His life for us He gives;
'I choose you, give your life as one for the other lives'

God's Heart dwells among us, He longs for our hearts: no sin
The Heart of His home knocks our door, pounding to come in
With every lasting beat, His Heart pounds passion's pure love
Louder and louder it pounds, pelting our hearts whereof

Poem: *The Vinedresser, The Vine, The Branch* (John 15: 1–8)

Ah, such refreshment we receive from Jesus' nourishing presence
He leads our way and sustains us by His life-giving, holy essence
I taste of His provisions, never feeling that my strength is waning
He alone is our Source, Food, and Life: within Him our fount sustaining

He lives as the Vine feeding its branches, so in us abundance thrives
Abiding in Him, we become His branches that He alone revives
By abiding in His Source from God, the Vine refills our endless fount
By remaining branches of His Vine, we our circumstances surmount

Always abide and never sever the communion of branch and Vine
Apart from Him, we suffer thirst and wither, in a swift, parched decline
Being parched, we become useless in producing bountiful fresh fruit
God will gather the useless branches and by fire He'll thus refute

Remain the branches with Jesus, the Vine, that God, our Vinedresser sent
In fruitfulness, you then, shall produce all the Vine and Vinedresser spent
for you to commune with Him for sustenance to grow strong and remain
growing secure, thriving upon His Vine, for others to thus sustain

At times, you may feel the sharp pinch of the Vinedresser's loving, trimmed
care
For He prunes those who are fruitful, so that more fruitfulness they may bear
Do not be dismayed by His pruning touch, for in such His great love lives
that we can become all that we should, as from His hand, rich life He gives

If severed from Christ's nourishing Vine, our lifeless branch in death will fall
and fail to survive to the holy time when Christs' trumpet blows His call
If severed we stay apart from His Vine—we stoke our own inferno
Our wasted lives, heaps of ashes in rows, devoid of God's blessed furrow

Christ alone is our Source, Food, and Life, within Him our fount sustaining
An endless supply of rich food for life; ask for your needs maintaining
Ask in His name and He will provide all that abundance requires
If you abide in Him and Him in you, He'll give you your desires

He lives as the Vine feeding its branches, so in us abundance thrives
Abiding in Him, we become His branches that He alone revives
By abiding in His Source from God, the Vine refills our endless fount
By remaining branches of His Vine, we our circumstances surmount

Ah, such refreshment we receive from Jesus' nourishing presence
He leads our way and sustains us by His life-giving, holy essence
I taste of His provisions, never feeling that my strength is waning
He alone is our Source, Food, and Life: within Him our fount sustaining

Poem: *Purple Heart* (John 15: 11–17; 16: 12–15, 19–24, 33)

How purple His Heart that He beckons us take His life's vital offer
of All of Himself, all that he owns: replete from God's Royal Coffer
What love is this that gives us His all without a costly condition?
We only must ask for what is His with heartfelt, humble submission!

Jesus says: 'What is mine is yours, I declare it to you: the Father gives it all
Believe in Me, then the Spirit of Truth will upon your ears thus fall
He will glorify Me and tell you of the amazing things to come,
imparting what you need to hear, becoming wise and richly wholesome

In a little while, you will not see Me—then, you will see Me return
Sorrow will rob your hearts of joy as for My presence again you yearn
Then, joy will increase your bounty once more, as my presence reappears
This joy can never be taken away—not by man and not by years

In that day of My going away, you will ask nothing in My name
But, with the day of returning joy, My Heart you will ask to reclaim
At your joyous reclamation, you will ask My Father in My name
to give you more of Me through Him, so with Our Spirit, your joy sustain

My Purple Heart of sacred love and life, will fulfill your every need
You will partake of my holiness, while God's pure love becomes your creed
Take My Heart's color purple for the tincture of your new heart's passion
Render your life to the heartfelt joy of My Purple Heart's compassion'

How purple His Heart that He beckons us take His life's vital offer
of All of Himself, all that he owns: replete from God's Royal Coffer
What love is this that gives us His all without a costly condition?
We only must ask for what is His with heartfelt, humble submission!
Ask in His Name with His joy in your life, and receive His Purple Heart!

God Gives Himself, His Son, His Spirit: His Royal Coffer of Love

We have traveled an amazingly long way on this highly-blessed road with Jesus and His Apostles! Now, Jesus has taken a 'timeout' from His identity as our tour guide, teacher, and friend to pray to God, His heavenly Father. He's not far away, though; and, we are within earshot of His prayers, which we will reflect upon later. Surely, if we keep at least one ear in his direction as He prays, we will learn more from Him and become much wiser, still, about God's Heart! Remember, when we began down this road, He said that He would never leave us or forsake us along the way. So, no worries on getting left behind and lost! Just keep actively listening for His voice and peacefully resting in His nearby presence.

But, as we rest, let's sit and also savor, digest, and process into our lives the application of what Jesus told us since our last rest stop…

As I heard Him, dear friends, He said:

- that He is the Son of God, the True Bread of Life, and that all who believe in Him will always secure all their needs through a faithful belief in Him and following of His way;
- that when we seek God with ALL our hearts, we WILL find the One True God and His Heart;
- that when we know Him (Jesus), we thus find and know our Father God in heaven because God sent Him to show us the Father;

- that He came in obedience to God unto death on the Cross, so that we may live;

- **that God longs, with more passion than we can ever humanly imagine, for us to come to Him, follow Him and abide in Him, intimately know Him, and enjoy His Holy Presence with all the love He has to give, along with all the provisions He owns** (which is EVERYTHING in existence), and the everlasting life that He freely offers;

- that God FERVENTLY LONGS for us to be One with Him and Jesus (as They are One) so that we can be bountifully blessed and favored; and then, as His faithful, fruitful, and obedient servants, pass the blessings along to others;

- that once we are His, we never separate ourselves from Him by caving-in to our former worldly ways; but, that we remain always connected to Him (Jesus) and the Father in heaven to thrive and secure everlasting life with Them;

- that He (Jesus) is going away; but, upon leaving, He will send the Holy Spirit (the 'Spirit of Truth') to abide with us to teach us and give us all knowledge that we seek, guide us, comfort us, bring us peace, and love us beyond all measure until He returns!

- that though He is going away, and we will not see Him for a while, which will bring such sorrow to our hearts so that we will make no requests in His name, He will never really leave us;

- that He WILL return to us, bring joy to our hearts once again, if we ask for Him to be in our lives. At that time when joyously sharing life with Him, we will joyously ask all things in His name and will receive;

- that He is the Truth, the Life, and the Way to God's loving Heart; and,

- that all we have to do is to take **His freely-given, vital offer of eternal life through belief in Him, Jesus Christ – God's only begotten Son, to find and share all the secrets of God's Heart's treasures!**

I scarcely can comprehend all that! What are your thoughts, on His words, fellow travelers? Let's take time to mull over and fully grasp the meaning of His recent words! **Surely, they are promises because He always speaks the Truth!** So, along with everything else Jesus formerly taught and showed us along the way, let's discuss His new words. Let's add to our knowledge and allow them to collaboratively sink with the rest of His teachings deeply into our hearts, minds, and souls. We have time to think about this because Jesus is still praying.

I would paraphrase Jesus as follows:

All we have to do is believe in Jesus as God's only begotten and freely-given Son, the Christ, *Who is our Lord and Savior, fully receive Him, truly love Him, faithfully believe in His teachings, earnestly follow Him, joyously honor and adore Him, steadfastly obey Him, humbly serve Him, and willfully stay connected to Him and God for us to inherit all those promises?*

Do you agree? What do you think? It seems that He only asks for our faithfully believing and sincerely loving hearts in return for all His promises of blessings, favors, grace, and eternal life with Him along with His inexhaustible provisions and care. I'm thoroughly amazed! How about you? Again, I scarcely can take it all in!

In a nutshell, He only wants our acceptance, belief, willful and faithful connectivity, and surrendered, respectful love in order to gain everlasting life with Him and all that He provides! Of course, additionally, He would like our intense discipleship, never-failing obedience, and fervent service, too! But, out of His magnanimously offered and freely given fatherly love (His Father's Heart), He overlooks many of our shortcomings, not making them requirements—just icing on His cake of eternal existence. It is overwhelming to fathom that kind of love, is it not? He asks for nothing but our hearts, but gives us everything forever from His Heart in return!

Now, let's also reflect on Jesus' nearby prayers that we overheard as we rested. Surely, He richly blessed us again with His unimaginable heart of love. Remember, He, firstly, prayed for His Disciples. Secondly, He prayed for ALL BELIEVERS and the world! Wow! I think that means everyone who believes in Him for all time! That means us and everyone who comes after us forever! That also means that besides being our guide, teacher, and friend, Jesus is also our prayer Intercessor to God Almighty in heaven. Out of the abundance of His love, Jesus deeply cares for us and all creation! He is passionately concerned about humanity's well-being now and for all eternity! That is

AMAZING LOVE AND GRACE! That is unfathomable giving! That is the best gift of His heart to faithful disciples and believers for all time! How can our limited minds ever fully understand a loving heart so passionately great? Also remember, Jesus is God on earth, so His passionate prayers express the Heart of Almighty God.

Because God deeply cares for us, let's try with as much ability as we can muster to grasp the depth of God's loving heart through His prayers! We don't want to change His words, we just want to discuss them in our own terms, right? We just want to give His words real life application for our earthly existence. His prayers requested blessings for His Disciples, us, and the world. With the guidance of God's Holy Spirit, I express them in the following poems:

Poem: *Holy Precant* (Jesus Prays for His Disciples: John 17: 6–15, 17–19)

'Holy Father, hear My prayer from Your Heart
You are the One Truth that I plead impart
to the men you gave Me in this brash world
I am Yours, We are One Truth, purely pearled

That I speak Your Truth, they strongly cherish
When I come to You, pray none should perish
The men receive and believe all from Me:
All that You gave Me in Your sanctity

They are now Mine, I am as ever Yours
I kept them for You; Our Oneness secures
their safekeeping with Us, while I must leave
Joy to them, as My joy to themselves cleave

Holy Father, hear My prayer from Your Heart
You are the One Truth that I plead impart
Stay with them here, while to You I must go
Give them all they need to have and to know

No longer of the world, for them I pray

Truth within themselves by night and by day
As tender shoots from Truth's crops newly born,
No longer of the world, Truth they adorn

Take them not from the world, let them here stay
Protect them from evil along their way
None must be lost, but, tended with Your care
My Father, keep them safe from evil's snare

The Son of Perdition is firmly lost
He will receive his price; his life be tossed
to Scripture's fulfillment and upheld end
To Satan he must go; to Satan send!

As for the rest, I have already sent
them into the world, preaching all you spent
from My birth to the Cross, that some be well
They must go to the world and of Us tell

I am sanctified by You, and so they
I pray for them and for their lives to stay
One with Us as We are One sanctity:
Inviolable Truth—the world need see

Holy Father, hear My prayer from Your Heart
You are the One Truth that I plead impart
to the men you gave Me in this brash world
I am Yours, We are One Truth, now unfurled

Holy Father, hear My prayer of Truth One!
Holy Father, hear My prayer for Truth won!'

Poem: *Merciful Inclusion* **(Jesus Prays for All Believers: John 17: 20–26)**

How great our Lord that He now prays for our future existence
Merciful inclusion in His love by prayerful persistence
He sees our lives pure and holy as only He purely shall
Prayerful inclusion of love from His merciful heart's locale

He not only prays to intercede for the saved Eleven
He also prays believers through them shall join all in heaven
Such a mercy He proclaims from His heart of hot gilded gold
No greater love, passion, and concern than this from His lips told

He says He wants us One with Him and His Heavenly Father
He says we should not be left behind—parted, lost, but rather:
He gave us His glory with all rights to His Holy Kingdom,
One with Him forevermore, knowing His Heart's vast dominion

Jesus, Jesus, no other heart could so lovingly request
Our Oneness with Him and The Father, by His prayerful behest
Come now, we come, receiving His Royal, pure invitation
He made us One with Him, loved by The Father of creation

How great our Lord that He now prays for our future existence
Merciful inclusion in His love by prayerful persistence
Such a mercy He proclaims from His heart of hot gilded gold!
No greater love, passion, and concern than this from His lips told!

Christ's hot, gilded heart of gold; oh, blessed merciful inclusion!

Merciful and Inclusive, Holy Precant

Having witnessed Jesus' wondrous miracles, having heard and received His passionate sermons, having heard in His prayers His heart's blazing desires and cares for our well-being and the world's saving, having accepted His blessings and promises for all time, having been shown the way to truth and life, and having seen His holiness personified before our very eyes, we can continue the rest of our travel with the Apostle John in faith, confidence, hope, and trust. We now know that everything will be okay. We now have no fear of the journey with Christ as our guide. Jesus will protect and save us, no matter what! Now, we feel entirely and completely loved by Jesus, thus God Himself! The long journey and search for God's Heart will end the way that it should—safely and securely in Jesus' eternally burning love!

Now, get ready, we're off again after Jesus finished praying. He is on the move again. He is leading us across the Brook of Kidron to the olive grove overlooking the eastern wall of Jerusalem. He is taking all of His Apostles, minus Judas Iscariot, into the garden.[9] Let's keep following in hope and trust

---

[9] https: //www.israeladvantagetours.com/: "Known in **Scripture** only as 'the **brook Kidron,'** the **Kidron** Valley runs north to south between the Mount of Olives and the eastern wall of the Temple Mount. The 20-mile long stretch naturally descends 4,000 feet and tapers off into the Dead Sea. It was in this valley where King Jehoshaphat is

that we will finally find the full measure of God's Heart in the garden with Jesus.

Poem: *Drink from the Cup* (John 18: 1–11)

Drink from the cup, the journey's Way welcomes all who know thirst
Drink from His cup, this is the last stop, offered by the First
Christ has suffered long for our keeping, and bids us partake
by way of the Will of The Father Who's cup, we should take

Jesus offered His all, now He lets sin's nature attest
to the Will of the Father Who by our sin we are blessed!
We must follow Him to share sin's painful way to its snare
We will find Jesus' keeping, lifted up for us there

By Judas betrayed, Jesus welcomes sin's merciless Cross
He proclaims the Will of The Father to redeem sin's loss
The Way to the Cross cries out, 'sin's captured hold cannot stand!'
Jesus calls, 'The Way bears My cup's drink, peace be My command!'

Though betrayed by Judas to the law's hands in the garden
Jesus gave His life for us, not seeking any pardon
Forward, He surrendered life with love's willful strong heartbeat,
nailing Himself to the Cross: His blood brought evil's defeat

Jesus, the Christ, our Savior, filled our cups with His shed blood
so, the thirsty can drink and honor how Love strongly stood:
nailed to the Cross, defeating evil's stronghold called the earth
Drink from Love's blood-filled cup, cherish His Heart's gift of rebirth

---

thought to have overthrown the enemies of Israel (2 Chr. 20: 26). King David fled through the **Kidron** Valley during the rebellion of Absalom (2 Samuel 15: 23)."

We must follow Him to the staked Cross—share sin's woeful cost!
We will find Jesus there, lifted up for all who are lost
The Cross of Jesus defeated our journey's painful turns
He awaits us all there where His blazing Heart for us yearns

Drink from the cup, the journey's Way welcomes all who know thirst
Drink from His cup, this is the peace offering by the First
Christ suffered the Cross and bids of His power we partake
for the way to The Father's Heart where Love lives for our sake

Drink from the cup, the journey's Way welcomes all who know thirst
Drink from His cup, the last drop quenches our thirst by the First
Christ has suffered long for our keeping, and bids us partake
by way of the Will of The Father Who's cup we must take!

Drink from The Cup!

Drink from The Cup

In the garden, we find more than expected. We were searching for the full
measure of God's Heart through Jesus. We found a portion so big that it defies
human understanding: Jesus wholeheartedly surrendered Himself under arrest
to the Romans, Pharisees, and chief priests. Judas Iscariot, the absent Apostle,
led them to Him and kissed Jesus on the cheek to deceitfully identify Him to
the soldiers. **Jesus willingly said, "I am He, the One you want. Let all the**

others go." Jesus gave up Himself for all others so that they could live and be saved! Now, that is an amazing love coming from an intensely passionate and flaming heart! Can we love like that?

Our journey painfully led us to a place where we never imagined going. Jesus is carrying a large wooden cross on His beaten and ripped back as He stumbles up a path to a pre-appointed rocky hillside. They are taking Jesus to Golgotha (Calvary, the Skull) to be crucified on that wooden Cross before the whole world. But what are His sins? What did He do to deserve this? Why must He be treated like a criminal? If anyone is perfect, pure, and holy, surely, it is He! I cannot bear to witness this tragedy! It causes too much suffering, too much pain!

Upon being nailed to the Cross, **Jesus asked God the Father to forgive everyone: "Father, forgive them, for they do not know what they do."**[10]. And, after the complete infliction of extreme brutality and horrific crucifixion, **Jesus cried out: "It is finished!"** He is now dead. His lifeless and torn body remains before us. Can we ever fathom the meaning of such barbarism alongside His precious last words to mankind? How does vicious inhumanity and overwhelming Godly love meet in the same place on the Cross firmly planted in a rocky hillside? Jesus spoke words of forgiveness for His cruelest enemies.

Jesus spoke as if His purpose for living hung with Him on that Cross. Who would purposefully surrender to His own crucifixion? Who could bring their heart to forgive such brutality? For what purpose would He hang there in apparent brokenness and utter defeat for all to see? I cannot humanly understand mankind's cruelty in exchange for Pure Love!

This is not our journey's end. Jesus will not leave us in despair at His death on the Cross. **The torture of the Cross reveals His heart's treasure, which we are seeking!** This is not the end! Friends, there is more. He is off the Cross!

---

[10] Luke 23: 34, "Then Jesus said, 'Father, forgive them, for they do not know what they do.'"

Poem: *The Rock Garden* (John 19: 17–30)

Come to the garden, a Crossed tree planted and rooted in The Rock
Where evil and Truth collide for the holy meeting of His flock
There's no crookedness lingering there, though warped spirits dug the hole
and planted the Cross that raised up Jesus and nailed Him to that pole

Come to the Garden, grown from tilled Rock on Golgotha's dark hillside
Where evil tried to put Truth to death as the forces did collide
Evil was brutal: fiercely fought his battle of bloodthirsty force
Truth and Purity defeated the blows: conviction as His source

Come to the garden; Jesus is the Rock, born to die for our sins
The Rock, Pure Jesus, died on the Cross for sins indulgence to cleanse
It makes no sense that Purity should die to dampen sin's foul growth
But, through death, Pure Jesus redeems the blooms that evil once soweth

Come to the Garden, where roots dig deep to support the Rock's firm hands
Jesus is the Rock, accept His grasp, and live firmly where He stands
He stands for Truth, He stands for Love, He stands for Holy Righteousness
He stands for Goodness, Faith, Joy, Peace, Justice, and complete Forgiveness

Come to the Garden; Jesus is the Gardner, born to cleanse our sins
The Gardner, Pure Jesus, toiled through death for sin's quenching to cleanse
Sin drank of His blood, quenched it's thirst, then died, as Purity must live
The Cross of Jesus, the birth of new growth, through the Gardner's blood give

Come to the garden; strongly share the love flowing from His True Heart
His passionate Heart, broken and torn, bidding the world to depart
from inherited ways grown from the garden where sin took command,
to the garden at the foot of the Cross, rooted to firmly stand

Come to the Garden; Jesus calls from His appointed and marked tree,
the rooted tree in the Rock, planted for all to witness and see
Jesus, the Christ, watering and feeding the tree with His shed blood
Evil's deadly blow brought new life where travesty's horror once stood

Come to the Garden, at the Rock, you will find fertile time for prayer
The Rock Garden of Christ: prayers free flowers picked and gathered there
Gather your bouquet with an aroma sweeter than imagined
displayed with Christ's Heart and by His copious wounds strongly fastened

Come to the Garden, in the rooted Rock, you will find identity
growing blooms in your life that only through His love sprout clarity
In His Garden, you find clear love, peace, mercy, strength, perseverance
The Cross of Christ: identify—share in His Holy appearance

Come to the Garden, in the rooted Rock, you will find your purpose
tending the abundant blossoms of life, grown in freedom's surplus
For in the rooted Rock, the Cross of Christ stands firm for one and all
When you come to the Rock Garden of Christ, you have answered His call

Come to the Garden; find God's Heart nailed to the Cross of redemption
Though reposed by sin's hand, His Heart does command graceful remission
Covet only His love that absolves dead blooms with bright fresh flowers
Come to the Garden on the Rock and indulge your finest hours

Come to the Garden; at the Rock, you will find God's vast wisdom
The Rock Garden of Christ: wisdom revealed from God's Holy Kingdom
God, alone, gives vast wisdom for life's bizarre, imposed dilemma
Jesus Christ, The Rock of the Cross, the Alpha and Omega

Imagine a garden dried up from the death of its finest blooms,
replenished by the Gardner's blood, releasing His choicest perfumes
Fumes for cleansing and restoring new life to blooms from sin's dead soil
Cleansing by the Gardner's hands, dripping the blood from Christ's Heart-
spent toil

Imagine Christ's Rock Garden and come!

Come to The Garden on The Rock

Poem: *He Still Loves Us* (John 18: 25–27; 20: 1–25; 21: 15–17)

He still loves us when we don't fully grasp
His presence in miracles, blessings past
When seeing Him escapes our woeful eyes,
God calls us with His love, in great surprise!

He still loves us when we deny His Name
Holy Love always there, remains the same
When serving Him causes us to claim fear
God claims us until we dare hold Him near

He still loves us when we doubt His True Word
Showing us His way, His voice we have heard
Showing us His Body as He arose
Now, raised from slumber's concluded repose

He still loves us when we decline to see,
when we fear His ways, or in great doubt be
Everlasting His love, never failing
Mercy, forgiveness, grace—love prevailing!
He still loves us!

(As a fitting poem to scripture found in John 20: 1–23, but derived from Luke 23, please read and feel the depth of God's love with His sacrifice at the Cross in my following poem, *His Body*, from my book, *The Gift of God's Word (2006)*).

Poem: *His Body* (Not in the Appendices: Luke 23: 32–55; 24: 1–49)

Oh Lord, tell me!

How was His body when from Him life was stripped?
Was He torn, was He mangled, was He bloodied and ripped?
Was He beautiful at heart as He hung torn and tattered?
Was He exuding forgiveness of sins though physically shattered?

Oh Lord, tell me!

How was His body when from disgrace they dropped Him down?
Was He limp, was He lifeless, was He still wearing His crown?
Was He peaceful at rest after suffering more than one should?
Was He looking back with fulfillment as we know that He would?

Oh Lord, tell me!

How was His body when they laid Him gently to rest?
Was He bathed, was He clothed, anointed and refreshed?
Were the stains still there from His accomplished pure deed?
Were the cuts and bruises unsightly? With passion, I plead!

Oh Lord, tell me!

How was His body when He arose and walked the third day?
Was He dressed well for our viewing in our minds to replay
that wondrous moment when He came back to save us from sin?
Oh, God, as He arose to behold Him, I plead again and again!

Oh Lord, tell me!

How was His body as He appeared to soothe His beloved believers?
Was He glowing with love and forgiveness for even the deceivers?
Was He fervent in love and forgiveness on His third day's return?
Could we all behold Him with love and from His suffering learn?

Oh Lord, tell me!

How was His body when He ascended to Your heavenly center?
Was He brightly magnificent in holiness prepared to heaven enter?
Was He clothed in purity and devotion, though stripped by our sin?
Was He wearing goodness and sanctity as He entered therein?

Oh Lord, tell me!

How was His body as You greeted Him when His task was done?
Was He shining magnificently far brighter than our noonday sun?
Or was He shadowed by sin's clothing that with duty He pressed?
Was He before You pure, holy, and in hallowed dressings blessed?

Oh Lord, tell me!

How is His body here on earth after He left us and ascended?
Are we bathed, are we clothed in goodness, and from all sin mended?
Are we weak, are we changed, are we in love and mercy glowing?
Are we cleansed, well-dressed, with His sacrifice to us bestowing?

Oh Lord, tell me!

How is His body here on earth after His Holy Spirit descended?
Are we joined in the Holy Spirit's power to make all sin ended?
Are we strong, are we forgiven with love and mercy glowing?
Are we cleansed, though He departed with His sacrifice to us bestowing?

Oh, Lord tell me!

How was His body?

Oh Lord, tell me!

How is His body?

How was His Body? How is His Body?

Poem: *The Emptied Fullness* (John 20: 1–23)

I am emptied in grief for I know the pain of having lost
Emptied by the loss of a child, loved ones gone, and in death tossed
Emptied by the loss of precious life that I once held so dear
Consoled by the Heart of our Father, and, lovingly brought near

Our Father in heaven lost His child when Christ hung on the Cross
He knows our pain; He knows our suffering from our deepest loss
The Father in heaven appreciates our deep, darkest grief:
He turned His face from viewing Christ's Cross in Holy disbelief

The Father in heaven, our God, Creator of life and death
could not behold death's indulgence on Christ—completely bereft!
It was God's darkest hour as His Son hung bloodied and torn
Sin's toll on God's Heart overshadowed His love: reserved to mourn!

But, then came the light of morning as Christ arose from the dead
Magnificent bright light filled the tomb, where Christ once laid His head
Christ emptied His tomb and filled it with the fullness of His light
Emptied, but, full with the light of new life, restored by God's might

Christ defeated sin's ugly death by emptying the dark tomb
As Jesus Christ arose from the dead, bright light replaced God's gloom
And so, with us, the empty tomb gives bright light for our new day
Hallelujah for the Risen One, He lights up our new way!

Now, I am filled with fresh hope; I know the light of a new day
The fullness of light in the emptied tomb shine's new life my way
The new life through Christ shines new life over my dark bereavement
The emptiness of my deepest loss, filled with Christ's achievement!

Believing in the Risen One, brings hope from gloom's possession
As the Father in heaven brought us hope, from death's transgression
The new hope we gain from The Risen Light of the emptied tomb
shines the new way to make Christ's light brightly replace our dark gloom

Look to the fullness of bright light shining from Christ's emptied tomb
There you will find joy and new life to replace your darkest gloom
Christ emptied His tomb and filled it with the fullness of His light
Emptied, but full, with the light of new life, restored by God's might

So, run from the tomb of your dark years to Christ's restoration
Find the fullness of life in the light of Christ's resurrection
Never again feel the darkness familiar from life's old start
Feel new hope, joy, peace, and favor; receive **The Light of God's Heart**

In grief and sorrow, look to **The Emptied Fullness** of Christ's tomb,
Find your restored full life and pure joy to replace your heart's gloom!
At the tomb, God's Heart welcomes you to receive Christ's bright new day
Hallelujah for the Risen One, The Light of our new way!

Hallelujah for The Emptied Fullness!
Hallelujah for the Risen Christ!

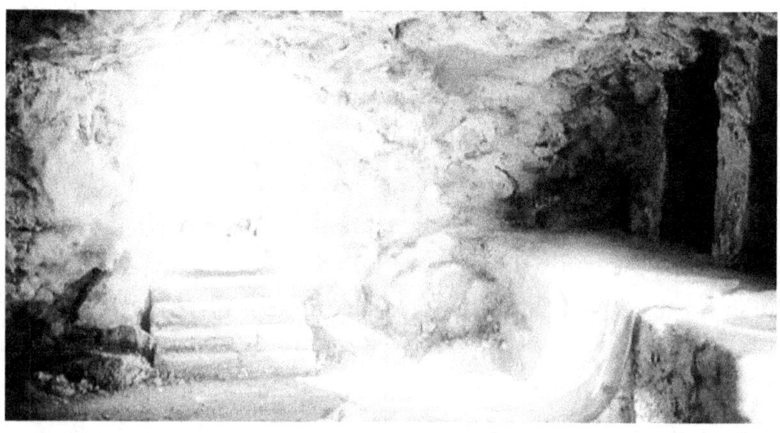

The Emptied Fullness of a New Day: The Light of God's Heart

Chapter V
Christ, God's Pure Heart: The Revealing of God through Christ, His Son

(*The First Epistle of John*, The Revelation of God Through Christ, His Son: Verses Found in Appendix E)

Earlier, we balked in disbelief at the treachery of Jesus' death on the Cross. But Jesus told us that He would rise again on the third day. And we wanted to know the truth! So, we stayed the course and followed John again. With John, we saw His empty tomb and all the evidence left behind: the tossed aside body wraps and the carefully folded and gently placed head covering. We saw Mary and Peter run to the empty tomb with John; and we witnessed their belief in the Risen Christ.

We heard the disciples speak about how Jesus suddenly appeared to them when they were meeting behind locked doors in post-crucifixion fear of the Pharisees. As He showed them His wounded hands and speared side, Jesus spoke, "Peace be with you. As the Father has sent me, so I send you." Then He breathed on them and said, "Receive the Holy Spirit. If you forgive anyone's sins, they are forgiven..."

Jesus' resurrection story actually came to life and is true! But this is not the end of our journey to find the treasure of God's Heart. Our search does not end at the empty tomb. The risen Christ will give us His Holy Spirit and power to do His Godly work, as well. God's Heart is more loving than we can ever imagine! We should keep seeking a while longer because Jesus may show us more. We have seen and heard so much! How much more than dying for our sins and raising from the dead to bring us new life will He do? I can only imagine!

Jesus is risen before us and is now calling us to go out with Him and His disciples to Bethany. Let's go! For sure, we will witness another miracle of the Lord in that place. We are following the Risen Christ!

As we watch, Jesus is stunningly ascending to heaven and blessing us as He goes. What greater love can we imagine? Truly, He is the Son of God! Let us fall down and worship Him and God, the Father in Heaven! God's love is so great and His Heart so Holy that He not only suffered and died on the Cross for us, but refused to leave us alone after Jesus' ascension to heaven! Through Jesus Christ, God gave us His Holy Spirit to live with and in us until the day of Christ's return. Through Jesus Christ, God gave us His heart. Now, great hope and joy live with us! God has given us beauty from the ashes (Isaiah 61)![11] How lovely! Through it all, God has given us His Spirit. We praise and worship You, dear Lord![12]

Poem: *Can We Rise That High* (1 John 1–5)

Can we rise with Christ to Light, Love, and Life
Know the depth of His Heart, leave behind strife
Know the sweetness of Life through His Pure Heart
Welcome Light, Life, and Love—in us be part

---

[11] Isaiah 61: 3, "To console those who mourn in Zion, To give them beauty for ashes, The oil of joy for mourning, The garment of praise for the spirit of heaviness;
That they may be called trees of righteousness, The planting of the Lord, that He may be glorified."

[12] Luke 24: 46–53: "Then He said to them, "Thus it is written, and thus it was necessary for the Christ to suffer and to rise from the dead the third day, and that repentance and remission of sins should be preached in His name to all nations, beginning at Jerusalem. And you are witnesses of these things. Behold, I send the Promise of My Father upon you; but tarry in the city of Jerusalem until you are endued with power from on high." And He led them out as far as Bethany, and He lifted up His hands and blessed them. Now it came to pass, while He blessed them, that He was parted from them and carried up into heaven. And they worshiped Him, and returned to Jerusalem with great joy, and were continually in the temple praising and blessing God. Amen." (Luke did not personally know Jesus or walk with Him in His lifetime. This is an accounting of the ascension as told to Luke by one of the eyewitnesses).

Can we rise to the heights with God to go
Bask in His merciful Light, all to know
Feel the flames of His Love from His stoked Heart
Stay eternally His, Life not to part

Can we escape the darkness, evade sin
Remain in His Light, show His Light to win
Light, Love, and Life for lost or called brothers
Win fellowship in Christ, loving others

Can we rise that high, touch Christ's bloodied feet
Sullied by sacrifice, Life's Love replete
Torn for all others as His life laid down
New life for us, redeemed under His Crown

Can we rise with Christ to lay down our lives
Give all for our friends, so new life revives
Love one another as God loved us first
Giving new Life through Christ to all who thirst

Can we rise that high, win eternal life
The prize of His Heart, ribboning our strife
He who has the Son, eternal life gain
The Son of God, Jesus Christ, bought our pain

Can we rise that high, touch the planted Cross
On the rock on the hill, redeem our loss
He hung there for all to receive His grace
See His Heart, touch His wounds, look face to face
in the eyes of our Savior, full of grace!

Can we see God live in ourselves today
Alive in us so we live truly—pray
He gave His Spirit as Christ ascended
Breathed new life in our souls, our sins mended

Can we rise that high, Christ ascended soared
To the highest bliss, seated with the Lord
Can we be like Him, love when hated
Forgive who hate us, vengeance abated

Can we rise with Christ to Light, Love, and Life
Know the depth of His Heart, leave behind strife
Know the sweetness of Life through His Pure Heart
Welcome Light, Life, and Love—never depart

Can we rise that high?

Can We Rise That High?

Poem: *How Lovely* (1 John 5: 1–5)

How lovely:

The mountain peaks aglow with white snow kissed
The daylight begun with fresh morning mist
The valleys alive with flowers and streams
The heavens spry with starlight and moonbeams

How lovely:

Waterfalls sketched with bright rainbow colors
Rock formations etched with stream-filled covers
A hungry bear waiting for fish to spawn
All of nature revived by each new dawn

How lovely:

The night's sky brilliance with moon, planets, stars
The comet's tail, the odd red tint of Mars
The ripples upon a hushed landscape's pond
The horizon's reach to land's far beyond

How lovely:

The forest trees in clustered oneness throng
The call of the Nightingale's hopeful song
The whisper of wind swiftly passing by
Sunsets tucking each day in the night's sky

How lovely:

Clustered white clouds set against the sky's blue
Fields topped with flowers of every known hue
Vista's reflections on the lake's bright face
Memories of joyful times never erased

How lovely:

Bright red and gold trees commencing the Fall
Leaves strewn about resounding winter's call
The chilliness of winter's day on cheeks
The peaceful fall of snow on hindered creeks

How lovely:

A huge crimson moon in the night's backdrop
Waves rushing to shorelines, never to stop
Waterfalls flowing to corralling pools
The dew stamped grass as temperature cools

How lovely:

Misty daylight beneath green forest trees
Birds airy flights o'er buzzing honey bees
Silhouetted trees on evening's repose
Stately oceans dressed in navy blue clothes

How lovely:

Fresh buds, new growth as spring kisses the air
Sweet, peaceful music on the yearning ear
Restful nights after a day's liveliness
Kisses from loved ones with a warm caress

How lovely:

All things provided by God's loving hand
All lovely things by God's loving command
Complete faith that God will always provide
The lovely things with which our lives collide

How Lovely!

How lovely is God! How lovely is He!
God is lovelier than all things we see!
He created all lovely things here known
All lovely things come from God's pure heart shown

How lovely!

How lovely is God! How lovely His Son!
Magnificence together as the One!
Jesus the Christ ascended to God's thrown
Lovelier by far over all things shown

How lovely!

How lovely is God! How lovely is He!
God is above all loveliness we see!
His loving, pure heart made all things for us
Honor Him, our Creator, glorious!

Glory be to God for all things lovely!
How lovely is He! Our Redeemer be:
How lovely! How lovely! How lovely—He!
How Lovely!

How Lovely!

Chapter VI
The Number of God's Perfect Heart of Love

(*Revelation* 1–22: John's Holy Vision, Verses Found in Appendix F)

I remain in awestruck silence of what I just witnessed! When we started this treasure hunt for God's Heart, never did I think that it could or would unravel truths like this. Truths that were capped with the Risen Christ ascending to heaven before our very eyes and blessing us as He went! But, even now, after all the happenings, signs, and miracles that we have seen along the journey, I hear the Apostle John speaking of unimaginable things to come, knowledge of which he received in a vision by an Angel of God. My mind is still processing the amazing and unfathomable loving events of our travels. Right now, it's difficult for me to hear and receive more of the wonders of God's Heart. At this juncture, however, my utmost desire urges me to continue this journey to the very end of which John speaks. Surely, we will be more deeply blessed and learn the 'unsearchable' things of which he speaks through revelation! Truly, there are just some things we cannot discover about God's Heart during our own earthly venture together. We must get the remainder straight from Almighty God! (Jeremiah 33: 3 – "I will answer you and show you great and unsearchable things of which you do not know.")

We know from John's revelation that one of the unsearchable things of which we do not know is that God will make all things new again. He will make a new heaven and new earth. A new garden of Eden, if you will. It will be a new heaven on earth where God again dwells with us, His people. God always wanted, and wants still, to be near to us and live among us. God wants to return the earth to its original, purity before sin dismantled His plan. God will make all things new and dwell with us once again. In our new home, there will be no more pain, tears, sorrow, or suffering. There will be no more death.

We will not suffer the second death placed upon those who reject Him at the end of the age. Our home with Him in the new heaven on the new earth will be just that—heavenly living for all eternity with our awesome Almighty God!

Let's, then, listen to the great and unsearchable things of which we do not know and continue the journey…

Poem: *Revelation Heart* (Revelation 1–22)

Unfathomable, unsearchable, Your wondrous heart to know
Almighty God, Your heart's endless, mysterious love to show
We fervidly know more must be, than what we see, hear, and touch
You revealed all in Your Word: Love, unimaginably such

Show us Your heart, Lord—reveal all things beyond our earthly grasp
Revelation of all things to come and all things of the past
For You are the One True Almighty God, Who makes all things new
Wondrous ways of holiness far beyond our limited view
Only You, only You, only You: Holy Three In One—You

Holy Creator, First Born, Everlasting, Powerful Might,
King of Kings, Majestic Three In One, Leading Star burning bright
Revealing all things through Your Spirit, surely to come from past
From the beginning of all time, from the first soul to the last

You make us kings and priests, washed by Christ's sacrifice at the Cross
You purely redeemed us through Your blood; while believing, not lost
Amazing grace, only You could regenerate our dead lives
Blessed mercy, Holy Love of Your heart, by which one survives

The Alpha, the Omega, the One returning on a cloud
Your trumpets will sound, Your angels resound, proclaim You aloud!
'Behold Him: King of Kings'—appearing to judge every nation,
every tribe and tongue, to the final breath in God's creation
And, at last, we all will bow in remorseful adoration!

His head and hair—white as wool, His eyes—red, flaming and fired
His feet shined like brass: from the Cross' glowing furnace—mired
His voice blasted like the great waterfalls thundering on earth
His right hand held all the churches proclaiming His Life and Worth

From His mouth, He wielded a double-edged sword: His Holy Word,
cutting the quick and the dead, severely slicing as they heard
Bright as a thousand suns He shone—ineffable sight to see
In fear, John bowed down to the ground, in reverence on bended knee

To the churches He holds in His hand, He warns where they have failed:
loveless, corrupt, fruitless, and lukewarm: no sincere act travailed
To the compromising and dead church—repent, change and be saved.
To the faithful and persecuted church—future not enslaved

Repentance of all brings mercy for all in loving, mixed ways:
Eat from the tree of life, death once not twice, no sword's thrust ablaze,
Earn power over all nations, clothed white in The Book of Life,
Stand a pillar in God's temple with God's name defeating strife

Zealously repent, open the door to His loving knocking
He will come in and dine with you, His heart's secrets unlocking
Repent, sit with Him on God's throne, feel His joy with your saving
His throne will be shared in love, as you lose the chains enslaving

Satan and Antichrist thrived a while before their painful end
Even knowing defeat would surely come, evil blows did send
over every man, every nation—to certain death beguiled,
save believers who accepted and proclaimed God's Holy Child

'Behold Him: King of Kings'—appearing to judge every nation,
We all will fearfully bow with remorseful adoration!
Praises to our heavenly God, mighty and true He judges
Seven Churches and all of the earth—with Seven bowls begrudges

Seven Spirits stand before His Throne, perfection at His feet
Fullness of wisdom is His alone, none on earth to compete
Worship the Lord, seek His counsel alone, mighty is His hand
He is all knowledge and understanding, bow at His command

Seven Beatitudes of salvation revealed in His Word
Wondrous promises to the faithful remaining as they heard
the Seven Trumpets sound, releasing the final blow to earth,
giving thanks to the crowned Holy One for His Almighty worth!

All praises to the Holy One, Seven Attributes He holds
Reining over all the world, His raining True judgment unfolds
'Behold Him: King of Kings'—appearing to judge every nation
We all will fearfully bow with remorseful adoration!

Almighty Everlasting King, You invite us up to see
a great tribulation for the ones, not bought, not Yours to be
Your blessed saints will not suffer the second death felt by the lost,
thrown into the cursed lake of fire, in lasting torture tossed

Faithful, loving, kind came You to save our world from deadly sin
The world rejected Your only Son and to the Cross did pin
For earthly souls who chose You and then, were ransomed by Your Grace
You return to save them once again to share Your holy space

Evil on the earth defeated, God on His Great Throne prevails
All glory to the King of Kings, 'Hallelujah'—all earth hails!
Glory, honor, and power to the One of the Trinity
Father, Son, and Holy Spirit, our God reigns in Unity!

Show us Your Heart, Lord—reveal all things beyond our earthly grasp
Revelation of all things to come and all things of the past
For You are the One True Almightily God, Who makes all things new
Wondrous ways of holiness far beyond our limited view
Only You, only You, only You: Holy Three In One—You

The Alpha, the Omega, the One returning on a cloud
Your trumpets will sound, your angels resound, proclaim You aloud!
'Behold Him: King of Kings'—appearing to judge every nation,
every tribe and tongue, to the final breath in God's creation
And, at last, we all will bow in remorseful adoration
Arias to the Kings of Kings, in wondrous proclamation!

Poem: *Revelation Seven* (Revelation 1–22)

Seven Spirits God possessed
Seven Churches warned and blessed
Seven Seals read in the scroll
Seven Trumpets to unfold

Seven Bowls Tribulations
Seven Judgments to nations
Seven sent for destruction
Seven spent for resumption

Seven Beatitudes wield
Blessings on believers yield
Blessings for the loving soul
Heeding prophecy of old

While all is lost, much is gained
Seven Blessings be sustained
Seven Beatitudes fall
On all who kneel to the call

Story of Seven complete
Perfect end through perfect feat
While all is lost, much is gained
Seven Blessings be sustained!

Poem: *Beatitudes Seven* (Revelation 1: 3; 14: 13; 16: 15; 19: 9; 20: 6; 22: 7; 22: 14)

Seven Beatitudes blessed
heeding hearts by love possessed
In seven verses revealed
Revelation—He will wield
Saved be you in His heart sealed!

1: 3—Blessings will he see
who reads, hears, heeds prophecy
The time is near to unfold
prophecy of books of old

14: 13—Blessed be one
who knows the Lord and His Son
upon his death from the earth,
rising to life in rebirth

16: 15—Blessed be he
who keeps with me harmony;
soils not his spirit's worth
with sin presiding on earth

19: 9—Blessings for one
dining with the Lamb, the Son
Invitation of the Lamb
Marriage seat by His command

20: 6—Blessed he will be
The second death, will not see
Raised with resurrection first,
one-thousand years reigning burst

22: 7—Blessed one
who heeds these Words, for I come
Quickly, I come to reclaim
My Church who I now rename

22: 14—Blessed be
who in white robes at His tree
will by the Tree of Life rest
Welcomed in at His behest

Seven Beatitudes blessed
heeding hearts by love possessed
In seven verses revealed
Revelation—He will wield
Saved be you in His heart sealed!

Poem: *Hallelujah Praises*

'Hallelujah' to the One on the throne
All creation is His and His alone
Praises we sing to the First and the Last
All things from Him, to Him, all things be cast!

God conquered evil, goodness will thus reign
Forever and ever, goodness remain
He loves us and can't forget us at last
Love's flaming red heart forgives us our past

Heaven sings praises to God on His Throne
Glory and honor from all called His own
The Saints and the Angels loudly profess
All glory to God, praise His Holiness

Glory Hallelujah, our One God reigns
Only by His love, our hearts He sustains
His Heart with our hearts, together will live
by His light, no night, His name He will give

'Hallelujah' to the One on the throne
All creation is His and His alone
Praises we sing to the First and the Last
All things from Him, to Him, all things be cast!
Glory, Hallelujah—our God forever reigns!

Poem: *Blessed Renewal*

Blessed be our Father Who brings heaven to earth,
despite all our failings and lack of our worth
He has renewed all things and our lives, as well
Blessed be our Father, unknown things not to tell

Blessed be the glimpse of the new heaven to come:
last vision of many, John sifted from some
God gave him on Patmos to bring us new life
Read the words, heed the warnings as God's new wife

Blessed be the bride of Jesus' new heaven,
formed from the saved of heeding churches seven
All who read, hear, believe, and receive will live
with Him, there in heaven, His Kingdom to give

Blessed be the land where God's gleaming heaven stand
It will sparkle with gem lights at God's command
The Alpha and Omega of all things true,
brings heaven to earth—creating all things new

Blessed be the light that shines bright from God's presence
The Holy Creator shines bright His essence
No night, no day to consume needless concerns
Simply life by His light that from His Heart burns

Blessed be God's heart, in hope, He yearns for us all
to come Home to His House despite our sad fall
He wants all to live with Him eternally
Blessed be God's heart, blessed be The One in Three

Blessed be His Throne, the Lamb of God there presides
All our tears, fears, cares wiped away by His side
The River of Life streams forth—the Throne it's start,
stretching out life's provisions to all impart

Blessed be the flow the River of Life sustains
Ripples of Life, Trees of Life, for us remains;
and the fruit of twelve kinds on each Tree springs forth,
yielding fresh fruit monthly, producing great worth

Blessed be the fruit, the Twelve Trees of Life sustain
Everything provided for those who remain
faithful, true, and worthy to the end of time
at the new earth's start—the new heaven sublime

Blessed be the Alpha, the Omega, our God
Beginning all things new with solely a nod
He loves us, He saves us, despite our failed past
He redeems us His own, of ones who would last

Blessed be His name, His eternal Holy name!
All things made new; nothing will remain the same!
Blessed be our Creator of the old and new!
Yes, His Heart bears all, for He lives to love you!

Blessed be our Father Who brings heaven to earth
despite all our failings and lack of our worth
He redeems us His own, He makes ALL things new
The Alpha and Omega of all things, True!

Poem: *The Story*

Have you read the story of the first and the last
from the first of all time to the last of time cast
In the beginning, He created from His Heart
In the end, redeemed the lost, with Him made a part!

God saw earth was good, which He spoke into being,
planted gardens with life, grand to His eyes seeing
And imagined creation, His perfect setting
With Adam and Eve's downfall—His Heart's regretting

How worthy, how worthy, God Almighty for us!
From all things fallen in sin, a renewal, thus
Hallelujah! Hallelujah! God, at last, reigns
By His hands He created; by His hands sustains

Praise to the eternal King Who Himself, He gave
His life for our lives, forever with Him, to save
Amazing grace, pure love from His breathtaking Heart
'It is finished,' He said, as from us did depart

Then returned, did He, to spread forth Love's True Story
Sending out disciples to tell of His glory
Calling all lost to share in His win at the Cross
Redeeming found souls: salvation restored by loss

All honor, glory, and praises to Jesus, Lord!
Holy of Holies, by His death all things restored!
Come to the Cross and receive His powerful love
Be restored by the power of redemption's Dove!

From redemption's Dove to the returning Lion,
destroying evil at the battle for Zion
Satan rendered to naught in blasphemy's mire
Satan and minions thrown in the Lake of Fire

Tribulation cost many lives, it's so foretold
In Revelation's Book to us, all best behold
Read and heed God's warnings revealed from His Pure Heart
warnings to overcome evil—gain a new start

A new heaven, a new earth restored from the last
God renews and restores, all lost things of the past
The earth and heavens remade: our lost lives reclaimed
We can live forever, His redeemed and renamed!

Oh, blessed is He, bless His Holy, Almighty Name!
We are the ones He lost, but, returned to reclaim
Praises to the Almighty One, great King of Kings
The newness of life from His impassioned Heart springs

Eternity knocks at our earthly broken doors
'Come to me,' He calls, as His blazing Heart implores:
'take My Hand, My Life, My Way, My Heart, and My Home;
take all that I have saved for the redeemed, alone!'

'For I am making again all creation new
Be the redeemed with Me; great stands My love for you
My Heart is burning with love's flame never dying
My love lasts forever for your heart's relying!'

A new heaven, a new earth restored from the last
God renews and restores all found things from the past
The earth and heavens remade; our found lives reclaimed
We can live forever, His redeemed and renamed!
Hallelujah, forever and ever, our gracious God and Savior reigns!

Poem: *How I Love You!*

I found the [one/One] my heart loves.
I held [him/Him] and I would not let go
(Song of Songs 3: 4)

How I love you, My fine and choice creation
My seed in My garden: a growing nation,
blossoming forth from My colorful planting,
covering pathways of old seed, supplanting

How I love you, My image in My garden
My walks with you, sweet memories of Eden
Even though fallen, in sin still lovely—fine
I love you as you are, because you are Mine

How I love you, planted by My Spirit's thought
Flowers so beautiful can't be thrown to naught
Even though dying, through pruning, blessed and true
My pruning of your stems brings growth of colors, new

How I love you—My True Pure Son, I sent
Offered for your saving, with great cost, I spent
He watered and refreshed your withering blooms
With His blood, new life gained that your life consumes

How I love you, My Apostles to you sent,
giving all My love to you from Christ's life spent
Boldly, vastly, they spread Good News of The Word,
quenching thirst for the Truth: in My Heart, preferred

How I love you, My Heart to you, through Christ give:
Eat of My Heart, drink My blood—deathlessly live!
Feast with Me at My Lamb's gracious wedding seat
Rejoice! Rejoice! Your saved lives with Me complete!

How I love you, give you My strength for each day,
directions for life, rough trials correcting your way
All given to you from My trunk, marked Pure Love
Angels sent your way, too, to help from above

How I love you, future warnings to John, spoke
Release yourself from the world, with Me be yoked
No greater love than Mine offered from My Heart
Feel My Heart's burning love, blazing from the start

How I love you, precious one, seek Me and find
all the treasures of My Heart, Purely Divine
Open My endless Heart with the keys of Christ
Stay with Me for your life, by My Heart enticed!

You have found Me! How I love you, child of mine!

How I love You, Father; loved You from the start
My love grows rich in the garden of Your Heart
You accept me though I need Your pruning touch
I love You, Father Dear, I love You so much!

How I love You, Father, for You first loved me
You came down to the ground—were nailed to The Tree
You rose again as You said, emptied the grave,
took the keys to hell's gate for our lives to save

How I love You, Father, with Your Heart, so dear
You saved me and held me, eternally near
Thank You for You, Your Son, and Holy Spirit!
You are The One Truth, giving life clear merit!

How I love you, Father; prize Your protection,
guiding my path of life, though through correction
I cherish Your Faithful Heart, Your True Spirit,
Your penned Living Word—I run to stay near it

How I love You, Father, Your warnings, I heed
in Your last book told, supplying our last need
I sought Your Heart; I found a treasure instead:
golden promises of love, by Your Heart fed

How I love You, Father, my life, I give You
Holy, loving Father, most steadfastly True!
You gave me Your life in exchange for my death
Your gracious love so great in depth, height, and breadth

How I love you, Father, Your Heart endearing
From my heart to Yours, endless love appearing
No greater love than mine, offered from my heart
Feel my heart's burning love, blazing from the start!

How I love You, Father; loved You from the start
My love grows rich in the garden of Your Heart
You accept me though I need Your pruning touch
I love You, Father Dear, I love You so much!

I found You! How I love you, Father of mine!

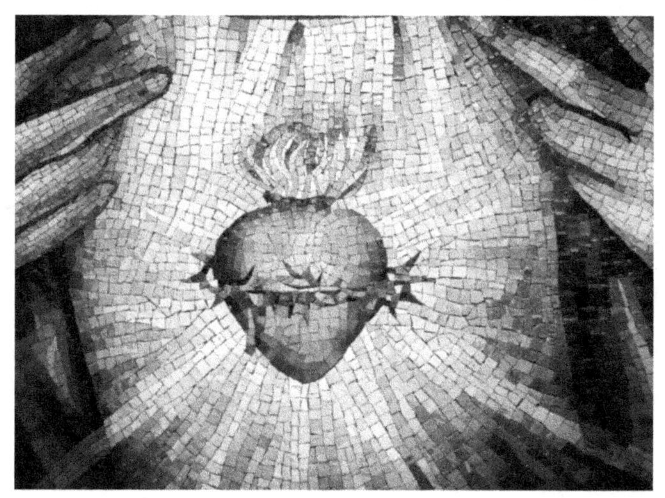

HOW I LOVE YOU!

Epilogue

Let's reflect on God's Word, which is the divinely inspired expression of His heart: *In the beginning...God created...and saw that it was good...*(Genesis 1: 1–31). That chapter in the Bible, alone, tells us that God created everything for our goodness, He gave us His loving heart's work, His creation, with the big, generous, and hopeful heart of the Father. And then, when we historically gave Him no reason to love or hope for us any longer, God again gave us Himself to redeem us. He humbly came into our decadent world in the flesh, as the perfect, sinless Jesus Christ, in the hope that we would learn how to love and live. He humbled Himself on earth to give us one last chance to receive His heart's love and join Him forever in His heart's home. Amazing, isn't it!

Think about it! An omnipotent, omniscient, omnipresent, and pure God, the Father of everything, freely gave us His loving work of creation; and then, when we had made an astronomical mess of it and didn't deserve His love at all (we were 'utterly helpless'), He gave us Himself unto death on the Cross for our atonement! He could have snuffed us out in an instant and written us off from His further plans. But He didn't!

"In the beginning..." God wrote us into His life's eternal plan by His loving Word. As a faithful Father Who is true to His Word, God kept His historical promises to keep with Him forever those who love Him in return. Can we love like that? That's what our lives are all about, dear friends: receiving God's love, living in God's love, and, thus, giving it back to Him and to others! We are offered a last chance to receive God's pure, loving heart as a freely given gift and share it with others. When others receive our love, as the Father in heaven freely gives, we are taking the right path to His heart. We are taking the right path home. We are receiving and re-gifting, if you will, God's heart.

When God, in perfect love, created the world, He gave us His heart; when He revealed to us his commandments, Covenants, and prophetic warnings, He gave us His heart; when He corrected our shortcomings with discipline, He gave us His heart; when He sent His only begotten Son, Jesus Christ, to die on His sacrificial Cross, He gave us His heart; when He gave us His Holy Spirit and His inerrant and everlasting written Word through His prophets and Apostles, He gave us His heart. Before all, in all, through all, and after all, God gave us His heart! He gave us His Heart of Love!

Yes, after all was accomplished at the Cross, God, in consummation, sent and gave His Holy Spirit as an everlasting way to His heart, which culminates to an everlasting home with Him. God's ways are truly not our humanly ways that fall so short of perfection. But God the heavenly Father 'created' a pathway for us to follow just so that we could find our way to His heart. Oh, that we should see His heart, no matter how far down life's path, and find our way to His heart's home! We don't have to be complete or holy. We just have to follow His divine path home. We just have to seek and find His completely perfect love! Then, we will have found His gift, His heart!

God's heart IS His gift! It is a sacred heart beyond human understanding or flesh-driven thoughts. Even so, God's beautiful gift of His heart, is accessible if we seek it, find it, receive it, live in it, and share it. We don't have to understand it. Like our own children, we are His children who don't have to deserve it. We just have to seek, find, receive, and act upon what is freely given. Then, we will start down the road to the wondrous love that partakes in the heavenly Father's sacred celebration of life, which comes with *The Gift of God's Heart.* His ultimate promise in **John 14: 21–23** is that **He will make His gift of His heart at home in our hearts.** Thus, at that time, our seeking journey for His heart becomes short, indeed! We will never have to travel far again to find Him. He will reside in us. We will have and hold His heart! We, therefore, will forever walk in His shoes! We will forever have a heartbeat that receives it's pacemaker from God, Himself.

Jesus searched His own heart when He started His arduous, painful journey toward our salvation, the finish line. He knew His purpose (to save and restore His garden of creation and ALL in it) and He examined what it would take to accomplish it to the end. In Luke 14: 28, Jesus admonishes us:

Which of you intending to build a tower, does not sit down first and count the cost, whether he has enough to finish it…

Let us search our hearts, as well. Do we have enough to finish the journey to God's Heart with Jesus, and then, with our lives build a tower of worship to Almighty God? Dear friends, we do! God did not leave Jesus alone when He surrendered to God's Will in Gethsemane. And Jesus has already made the way for us. All we have to do, now, is look to Him, receive Him, and follow His way. Our journey is now short. Our cost is already paid. Our tower is already in place. Everything that we need is already established for us. Now, put your own shoes back on. Walk alongside Jesus the rest of the way. Having found and received God's heart to cherish and share with others, you have all you need. You, thus, have 'enough to finish it'! (Luke 14: 28)

We have found You, Father God. We will hold You and not let go! (Songs of Songs 3: 4)

My Closing Prayer for Us All

As I thank God for all His grace, mercy, forgiveness, and goodness, my prayer is that we all will join God's celebration of renewed life, walk with Him, receive and appreciate the gift of His loving heart; and, let God's heart be the pacemaker of our own. I pray that we, then, will share His endless, immeasurable, and unimaginable love with others. I pray that we would share it with everyone, even if we personally feel that they don't deserve it or are not our own family or children. I pray, dear friends, that we will seek His heart and find it when we search for Him with all our hearts. I pray that all our personal gardens will flourish and be fertile to grow fresh produce in abundant fruitfulness for the glory of His name! I pray that we will all live together in the security and peace of His Holy Spirit. Amen.

1 John 1: 7

But, if we walk in the light as He is in the light, we have fellowship with one another, and the blood of Jesus Christ, His Son, cleanses us from all sin.

Appendix: Bible Verses
Appendices A–F

Appendix A
Genesis

Genesis 1–6

'In the beginning, **God created** the heavens and the earth. The earth was without form, and void; and darkness was on the face of the deep. And the Spirit of God was hovering over the face of the waters. Then God said, *Let there be light;* and there was light. And God saw the light, that it was good; and God divided the light from the darkness. God called the light Day, and the darkness He called Night. So, the evening and the morning were the first day.' (Genesis 1: 1–5 NKJV)

'Then God said, "Let there be a firmament in the midst of the waters, and let it divide the waters from the waters." Thus, God made the firmament, and divided the waters which were under the firmament from the waters which were above the firmament; and it was so. And God called the firmament Heaven. So, the evening and the morning were the second day.' (Genesis 1: 6–8 NKJV)

'Then God said, "Let the waters under the heavens be gathered together into one place, and let the dry land appear"; and it was so. And God called the dry land Earth, and the gathering together of the waters He called Seas. And God saw that it was good. Then God said, "Let the earth bring forth grass, the herb that yields seed, and the fruit tree that yields fruit according to its kind, whose seed is in itself, on the earth"; and it was so. And the earth brought forth grass, the herb that yields seed according to its kind, and the tree that yields fruit, whose seed is in itself according to its kind. And God saw that it was good. So, the evening and the morning were the third day.' (Genesis 1: 9–13 NKJV)

'Then God said, "Let there be lights in the firmament of the heavens to divide the day from the night; and let them be for signs and seasons, and for days and years; and let them be for lights in the firmament of the heavens to give light on the earth"; and it was so…God set them in the firmament of the heavens to give light on the earth, and to rule over the day and over the night, and to divide the light from the darkness. And God saw that it was good. So, the evening and the morning were the fourth day.' (Genesis 1: 14–19 NKJV)

'Then God said, "Let the waters abound with an abundance of living creatures, and let birds fly above the earth across the face of the firmament of the heavens." So, God created great sea creatures and every living thing that moves, with which the waters abounded, according to their kind, and every winged bird according to its kind. And God saw that it was good. And God blessed them, saying, "Be fruitful and multiply, and fill the waters in the seas, and let birds multiply on the earth." So, the evening and the morning were the fifth day.' (Genesis 1: 20–23 NKJV)

'Then God said, "Let the earth bring forth the living creature according to its kind: cattle and creeping thing and beast of the earth, each according to its kind"; and it was so. And God made the beast of the earth according to its kind, cattle according to its kind, and everything that creeps on the earth according to its kind. And God saw that it was good. Then God said, "Let Us make man in Our image, according to Our likeness; let them have dominion over the fish of the sea, over the birds of the air, and over the cattle, over all the earth and over every creeping thing that creeps on the earth." So, God created man in His own image; in the image of God, He created him; male and female He created them.

Then God blessed them, and God said to them, "Be fruitful and multiply; fill the earth and subdue it; have dominion over the fish of the sea, over the birds of the air, and over every living thing that moves on the earth."

And God said, "See, I have given you every herb that yields seed which is on the face of all the earth, and every tree whose fruit yields seed; to you it shall be for food. Also, to every beast of the earth, to every bird of the air, and to everything that creeps on the earth, in which there is life, I have given every green herb for food"; and it was so. Then God saw everything that He had made, and indeed it was very good. So, the evening and the morning were the sixth day.' (Genesis 1: 24–31 NKJV)

'Thus, the heavens and the earth, and all the host of them, were finished. And on the seventh day, God ended His work which He had done, and He rested on the seventh day from all His work which He had done. Then God blessed the seventh day and sanctified it, because in it He rested from all His work which God had created and made.' (Genesis 2: 1–3 NKJV)

'And the LORD God formed man of the dust of the ground and breathed into his nostrils the breath of life; and man became a living being. The LORD God planted a garden eastward in Eden, and there He put the man whom He had formed. And out of the ground the LORD God made every tree grow that is pleasant to the sight and good for food. The tree of life was also in the midst of the garden, and the tree of the knowledge of good and evil. Now, a river went out of Eden to water the garden, and from there it parted and became four riverheads. The name of the first is Pishon; it is the one which skirts the whole land of Havilah, where there is gold. And the gold of that land is good. Bdellium and the onyx stone are there. The name of the second river is Gihon; it is the one which goes around the whole land of Cush. The name of the third river is Hiddekel; it is the one which goes toward the east of Assyria. The fourth river is the Euphrates.' (Genesis 2: 7–14 NKJV)

Then the LORD God took the man and put him in the garden of Eden to tend and keep it. And the LORD God commanded the man, saying, "Of every tree of the garden you may freely eat; but of the tree of the knowledge of good and evil you shall not eat, for in the day that you eat of it you shall surely die."

And the LORD God said, " It is not good that man should be alone; I will make him a helper comparable to him." Out of the ground, the LORD God formed every beast of the field and every bird of the air and brought them to Adam to see what he would call them. And whatever Adam called each living creature, that was its name.' (Genesis 2: 15–19)

'So, Adam gave names to all cattle, to the birds of the air, and to every beast of the field. But for Adam, there was not found a helper comparable to him. And the LORD God caused a deep sleep to fall on Adam, and he slept; and He took one of his ribs and closed up the flesh in its place. Then the rib which the LORD God had taken from man He made into a woman, and He brought her to the man. And Adam said, "This is now bone of my bones And flesh of my flesh; She shall be called Woman, Because she was taken out of Man." Therefore, a man shall leave his father and mother and be joined to his wife, and they shall become one flesh. And they were both naked, the man and his wife, and were not ashamed.' (Genesis 2: 20–25)

'Now, the serpent was more cunning than any beast of the field which the LORD God had made. And he said to the woman, "Has God indeed said, 'You shall not eat of every tree of the garden'?"

And the woman said to the serpent, "We may eat the fruit of the trees of the garden; but of the fruit of the tree, which is in the midst of the garden, God has said, 'You shall not eat it, nor shall you touch it, lest you die'."

Then the serpent said to the woman, "You will not surely die. For God knows that in the day you eat of it your eyes will be opened, and you will be like God, knowing good and evil." So, when the woman saw that the tree was good for food, that it was pleasant to the eyes, and a tree desirable to make one wise, she took of its fruit and ate. She also gave to her husband with her, and he ate. Then the eyes of both of them were opened, and they knew that they were naked; and they sewed fig leaves together and made themselves coverings.' (Genesis 3: 1–7 NKJV)

'And they heard the sound of the LORD God walking in the garden in the cool of the day, and Adam and his wife hid themselves from the presence of the LORD God among the trees of the garden. Then the LORD God called to Adam and said to him, "Where are you?"

So, he said, "I heard Your voice in the garden, and I was afraid because I was naked; and I hid myself."

And He said, "Who told you that you were naked? Have you eaten from the tree of which I commanded you that you should not eat?"

Then the man said, "The woman whom You gave to be with me, she gave me of the tree, and I ate."

And the LORD God said to the woman, "What is this you have done?"

The woman said, "The serpent deceived me, and I ate."' (Genesis 3: 8–13 NKJV)

'So, the LORD God said to the serpent, "Because you have done this, You are cursed more than all cattle, And more than every beast of the field; On your belly you shall go, And you shall eat dust All the days of your life. And I will put enmity between you and the woman, And between your seed and her Seed; He shall bruise your head, And you shall bruise His heel."

To the woman, He said, "I will greatly multiply your sorrow and your conception; In pain you shall bring forth children; Your desire shall be for your husband, And he shall rule over you."

Then to Adam, He said, "Because you have heeded the voice of your wife and have eaten from the tree of which I commanded you, saying, 'You shall not eat of it': *Cursed is the ground for your sake; In toil you shall eat of it All the days of your life. Both thorns and thistles it shall bring forth for you, And you shall eat the herb of the field. In the sweat of your face, you shall eat bread Till you return to the ground, For out of it you were taken; For dust you are, And to dust you shall return.*" (Genesis 3: 14–19 NKJV)

'And Adam called his wife's name Eve, because she was the mother of all living. Also, for Adam and his wife the LORD God made tunics of skin and clothed them. Then the LORD God said, "Behold, the man has become like one of Us, to know good and evil. And now, lest he put out his hand and take also of the tree of life, and eat, and live forever"—therefore, the LORD God sent him out of the garden of Eden to till the ground from which he was taken. So, He drove out the man; and He placed cherubim at the east of the garden of Eden, and a flaming sword which turned every way, to guard the way to the tree of life.' (Genesis 3: 20–24 NKJV)

'Now, Adam knew Eve his wife, and she conceived and bore Cain, and said, "I have acquired a man from the LORD." Then she bore again, this time, his brother, Abel. Now, Abel was a keeper of sheep, but Cain was a tiller of the ground. And in the process of time, it came to pass that Cain brought an offering of the fruit of the ground to the LORD. Abel also brought of the firstborn of his flock and of their fat. And the LORD respected Abel and his offering, but He did not respect Cain and his offering. And Cain was very angry, and his countenance fell.

So, the LORD said to Cain, "Why are you angry? And why has your countenance fallen? If you do well, will you not be accepted? And if you do not do well, sin lies at the door. And its desire is for you, but you should rule over it."' (Genesis 4: 1–7 NKJV)

'Now Cain talked with Abel his brother; and it came to pass, when they were in the field, that Cain rose up against Abel his brother and killed him. Then the LORD said to Cain, "Where is Abel, your brother?"

He said, "I do not know. Am I my brother's keeper?"

And He said, "What have you done? The voice of your brother's blood cries out to Me from the ground. So, now you are cursed from the earth, which has opened its mouth to receive your brother's blood from your hand. When you till the ground, it shall no longer yield its strength to you. A fugitive and a vagabond you shall be on the earth."

And Cain said to the LORD, "My punishment is greater than I can bear! Surely, You have driven me out this day from the face of the ground; I shall be hidden from Your face; I shall be a fugitive and a vagabond on the earth, and it will happen that anyone who finds me will kill me."

And the LORD said to him, "Therefore, whoever kills Cain, vengeance shall be taken on him sevenfold."

And the LORD set a mark on Cain, lest anyone finding him should kill him.' (Genesis 4: 8–15 NKJV)

'And Adam knew his wife again, and she bore a son and named him Seth, *For God has appointed another seed for me instead of Abel, whom Cain killed.* And as for Seth, to him also a son was born; and he named him Ē´nosh. Then men began to call on the name of the LORD.' (Genesis 4: 25–26 NKJV)

'Then the LORD saw that the wickedness of man was great in the earth, and that every intent of the thoughts of his heart was only evil continually. And the LORD was sorry that He had made man on the earth, and He was grieved in His heart. So, the LORD said, "I will destroy man whom I have created from the face of the earth, both man and beast, creeping thing and birds of the air, for I am sorry that I have made them." But Noah found grace in the eyes of the LORD. The earth also was corrupt before God, and the earth was filled with violence. So, God looked upon the earth, and indeed it was corrupt; for all flesh had corrupted their way on the earth. And God said to Noah, "The end of all flesh has come before Me, for the earth is filled with violence through them; and behold, I will destroy them with the earth."'

(Genesis 6: 5–8, 11–13 NKJV)

(To do righteousness and justice Is more acceptable to the LORD than sacrifice Proverbs 21: 3 NKJV)

Appendix B
Exodus

Exodus 16–23

And the LORD spoke to Moses, saying, "I have heard the complaints of the children of Israel. Speak to them, saying, 'At twilight, you shall eat meat, and in the morning you shall be filled with bread. And you shall know that I am the LORD your God.'" So, it was that quails came up at evening and covered the camp, and in the morning the dew lay all around the camp. And when the layer of dew lifted, there, on the surface of the wilderness, was a small round substance, as fine as frost on the ground.

So, when the children of Israel saw it, they said to one another, "What is it?" For they did not know what it was.

And Moses said to them, "This is the bread which the LORD has given you to eat. This is the thing which the LORD has commanded: 'Let every man gather it according to each one's need, one omer for each person, according to the number of persons; let every man take for those who are in his tent.'" Exodus 16: 11–16 NKJV

'And God spoke all these words, saying, "I am the LORD your God, who brought you of the land of Egypt, out of the house of bondage. You shall have no other gods before Me. You shall not make for yourself a carved image— any likeness of anything that is in heaven above, or that is in the earth beneath, or that is in the water under the earth; you shall not bow down to them nor serve them. For I, the LORD your God, am a jealous God, visiting the iniquity of the fathers upon the children to the third and fourth generations of those who hate Me, but showing mercy to thousands, to those who love Me and keep My commandments. You shall not take the name of the LORD your God in vain, for the LORD will not hold him guiltless who takes His name in vain."'

Exodus 20: 1–7 NKJV

"Six days, you shall labor and do all your work, but the seventh day is the Sabbath of the LORD your God. In it, you shall do no work: you, nor your son, nor your daughter, nor your male servant, nor your female servant, nor your cattle, nor your stranger who is within your gates." For, in six days, the LORD made the heavens and the earth, the sea, and all that is in them, and rested the seventh day. Therefore, the LORD blessed the Sabbath day and hallowed it.

"Honor your father and your mother, that your days may be long upon the land which the LORD your God is giving you. You shall not murder. You shall not commit adultery. You shall not steal. You shall not bear false witness against your neighbor. You shall not covet your neighbor's house; you shall not covet your neighbor's wife, nor his male servant, nor his female servant, nor his ox, nor his donkey, nor anything that is your neighbor's."

Exodus 20: 9–17 NKJV

"Behold, I send an angel before you to keep you in the way and to bring you into the place which I have prepared. Beware of Him and obey His voice; do not provoke Him, for He will not pardon your transgressions; for My name is in Him. But if you indeed obey His voice and do all that I speak, then I will be an enemy to your enemies and an adversary to your adversaries."

Exodus 23: 20–22 NKJV

Appendix C
The Synoptic Gospel of Matthew

(Matthew 1–27)

'Now, the birth of Jesus Christ was as follows: After His mother Mary was betrothed to Joseph, before they came together, she was found with child of the Holy Spirit.'

Matthew 1: 18 NKJV

But while he thought about these things, behold, an angel of the Lord appeared to him in a dream, saying, "Joseph, son of David, do not be afraid to take to you Mary your wife, for that which is conceived in her is of the Holy Spirit. And she will bring forth a Son, and you shall call His name JESUS, for He will save His people from their sins."

So, all this was done that it might be fulfilled which was spoken by the Lord through the prophet, saying, "Behold, the virgin shall be with child, and bear a Son, and they shall call His name Immanuel," which is translated, *God with us.*

Matthew 1: 20–23 NKJV

'And he came and dwelled in a city called Nazareth, that it might be fulfilled which was spoken by the prophets, "He shall be called a Nazarene."'

Matthew 2: 23 NKJV

In those days, John the Baptist came preaching in the wilderness of Judea, and saying, "Repent, for the kingdom of heaven is at hand!" For this is he who was spoken of by the prophet Isaiah, saying, "The voice of one crying in the wilderness: 'Prepare the way of the LORD; Make His paths straight.'"

Matthew 3: 1–3 NKJV

'Then Jesus came from Galilee to John at the Jordan to be baptized by him. And John tried to prevent Him, saying, "I need to be baptized by You, and are You coming to me?"

But Jesus answered and said to him, "Permit it to be so now, for thus it is fitting for us to fulfill all righteousness." Then he allowed Him. When He had been baptized, Jesus came up immediately from the water; and behold, the heavens were opened to Him, and He saw the Spirit of God descending like a dove and alighting upon Him. And suddenly a voice came from heaven, saying, "This is My beloved Son, in whom I am well pleased."'

Matthew 3: 13–17 NKJV

'Then Jesus came from Galilee to John at the Jordan to be baptized by him. And John tried to prevent Him, saying, "I need to be baptized by You, and are You coming to me?"

But Jesus answered and said to him, "Permit it to be so now, for thus it is fitting for us to fulfill all righteousness." Then he allowed Him. When He had been baptized, Jesus came up immediately from the water; and behold, the heavens were opened to Him, and He saw the Spirit of God descending like a dove and alighting upon Him. And suddenly a voice came from heaven, saying, "This is My beloved Son, in whom I am well pleased."'

Matthew 3: 13–17 NKJV

Then Jesus was led up by the Spirit into the wilderness to be tempted by the devil. And when He had fasted forty days and forty nights, afterward He was hungry. Now, when the tempter came to Him, he said, "If You are the Son of God, command that these stones become bread."

But He answered and said, "It is written, 'Man shall not live by bread alone, but by every word that proceeds from the mouth of God.'"

Matthew 4: 1–4 NKJV

Jesus Calls His Apostles and Begins His Sacred Journey (Matthew 4: 13–17, 18–22, 23–25; 9: 35–38)

'And leaving Nazareth, He came and dwelled in Capernaum, which is by the sea, in the regions of Zebulun and Naphtali, that it might be fulfilled which was spoken by Isaiah the prophet, saying, "The land of Zebulun and the land of Naphtali, By the way of the sea, beyond the Jordan, Galilee of the Gentiles:

The people who sat in darkness have seen a great light, And upon those who sat in the region and shadow of death Light has dawned."

From that time Jesus began to preach and to say, "Repent, for the kingdom of heaven is at hand.""

Matthew 4: 13–17 NKJV

"And Jesus, walking by the Sea of Galilee, saw two brothers, Simon called Peter, and Andrew his brother, casting a net into the sea; for they were fishermen. Then He said to them, "Follow Me, and I will make you fishers of men." They immediately left their nets and followed Him. Going on from there, He saw two other brothers, James the son of Zebedee, and John his brother, in the boat with Zebedee their father, mending their nets. He called them, and immediately they left the boat and their father, and followed Him."

Matthew 4: 18–22 NKJV

'And Jesus went about all Galilee, teaching in their synagogues, preaching the gospel of the kingdom, and healing all kinds of sickness and all kinds of disease among the people. Then His fame went throughout all Syria; and they brought to Him all sick people who were afflicted with various diseases and torments, and those who were demon-possessed, epileptics, and paralytics; and He healed them. Great multitudes followed Him—from Galilee, and from Decapolis, Jerusalem, Judea, and beyond the Jordan.'

Matthew 4: 23–25 NKJV

'Then Jesus went about all the cities and villages, teaching in their synagogues, preaching the gospel of the kingdom, and healing every sickness and every disease among the people. But when He saw the multitudes, He was moved with compassion for them, because they were weary and scattered, like sheep having no shepherd. Then He said to His disciples, "The harvest truly is plentiful, but the laborers are few. Therefore, pray the Lord of the harvest to send out laborers into His harvest.""

Matthew 9: 35–38 NKJV

'But when Jesus knew it, He withdrew from there. **And great multitudes followed Him, and He healed them all.** Yet He warned them not to make Him known, that it might be fulfilled which was spoken by Isaiah the prophet, saying, "Behold! My Servant whom I have chosen, My Beloved in whom My soul is well pleased"!'

(Matthew 12: 15–18 NKJV)

Matthew 5–6–7: The Beatitudes

'And seeing the multitudes, He went up on a mountain, and when He was seated His disciples came to Him. Then He opened His mouth and taught them, saying,

Matthew 5: 1–2 NKJV (Jesus Teaches the Beatitudes: a proclamation of His heart)

Blessed are the poor in spirit, For theirs is the kingdom of heaven. Blessed are those who mourn, For they shall be comforted. Blessed are the meek, For they shall inherit the earth. Blessed are those who hunger and thirst for righteousness, For they shall be filled. Blessed are the merciful, For they shall obtain mercy. Blessed are the pure in heart, For they shall see God. Blessed are the peacemakers, For they shall be called sons of God. Blessed are those who are persecuted for righteousness' sake, For theirs is the kingdom of heaven. Blessed are you when they revile and persecute you and say all kinds of evil against you falsely for My sake. Rejoice and be exceedingly glad, for great is your reward in heaven, for so they persecuted the prophets who were before you.

You are the salt of the earth; but if the salt loses its flavor, how shall it be seasoned? It is then good for nothing but to be thrown out and trampled underfoot by men. You are the light of the world. A city that is set on a hill cannot be hidden. Nor do they light a lamp and put it under a basket, but on a lampstand, and it gives light to all who are in the house. Let your light so shine before men, that they may see your good works and glorify your Father in heaven.

Do not think that I came to destroy the Law or the Prophets. I did not come to destroy but to fulfill. For assuredly, I say to you, till heaven and earth pass away, one jot or one tittle will by no means pass from the law till all is fulfilled. Whoever therefore breaks one of the least of these commandments, and teaches men so, shall be called least in the kingdom of heaven; but whoever does and teaches them, he shall be called great in the kingdom of heaven. For I say to you, that unless your righteousness exceeds the righteousness of the scribes and Pharisees, you will by no means enter the kingdom of heaven.

You have heard that it was said to those of old, 'You shall not murder, and whoever murders will be in danger of the judgment.' But I say to you that whoever is angry with his brother without a cause shall be in danger of the judgment. And whoever says to his brother, 'Raca!' shall be in danger of the council. But whoever says, 'You fool!' shall be in danger of hell fire. Therefore, if you bring your gift to the altar, and there remember that your brother has something against you, leave your gift there before the altar, and go your way. First be reconciled to your brother, and then come and offer your gift. Agree with your adversary quickly, while you are on the way with him, lest your adversary deliver you to the judge, the judge hand you over to the officer, and you be thrown into prison. Assuredly, I say to you, you will by no means get out of there till you have paid the last penny.

You have heard that it was said to those of old, 'You shall not commit adultery.' But I say to you that whoever looks at a woman to lust for her has already committed adultery with her in his heart. If your right eye causes you to sin, pluck it out and cast it from you; for it is more profitable for you that one of your members perish, than for your whole body to be cast into hell.

And if your right hand causes you to sin, cut it off and cast it from you; for it is more profitable for you that one of your members perish, than for your whole body to be cast into hell.

Furthermore, it has been said, 'Whoever divorces his wife, let him give her a certificate of divorce.' But I say to you that whoever divorces his wife for any reason except sexual immorality causes her to commit adultery; and whoever marries a woman who is divorced commits adultery.

Again, you have heard that it was said to those of old, 'You shall not swear falsely, but shall perform your oaths to the Lord.' But I say to you, do not swear at all: neither by heaven, for it is God's throne; nor by the earth, for it is His footstool; nor by Jerusalem, for it is the city of the great King. Nor shall you swear by your head, because you cannot make one hair white or black. But let your 'Yes' be 'Yes,' and your 'No,' 'No.' For whatever is more than these is from the evil one.

You have heard that it was said, 'An eye for an eye and a tooth for a tooth.' But I tell you not to resist an evil person. But whoever slaps you on your right cheek, turn the other to him also. If anyone wants to sue you and take away your tunic, let him have your cloak also. And whoever compels you to go one mile, go with him two. Give to him who asks you, and from him who wants to borrow from you do not turn away.

You have heard that it was said, 'You shall love your neighbor and hate your enemy.' But I say to you, love your enemies, bless those who curse you, do good to those who hate you, and pray for those who spitefully use you and persecute you, that you may be sons of your Father in heaven; for He makes His sun rise on the evil and on the good, and sends rain on the just and on the unjust. For if you love those who love you, what reward have you? Do not even the tax collectors do the same? And if you greet your brethren only, what do you do more than others? Do not even the tax collectors do so? Therefore, you shall be perfect, just as your Father in heaven is perfect.

(Matthew 5: 1–48; 6: 1–34; 7: 1–27)

Matthew 14: 6–33; 15: 32–38: The Feeding of Five-Thousand

'But when Herod's birthday was celebrated, the daughter of Herodias danced before them and pleased Herod. Therefore, he promised with an oath to give her whatever she might ask. So, she, having been prompted by her mother, said, "Give me John, the Baptist's head here on a platter."

And the king was sorry; nevertheless, because of the oaths and because of those who sat with him, he commanded it to be given to her. So, he sent and had John beheaded in prison. And his head was brought on a platter and given to the girl, and she brought it to her mother.

Then his disciples came and took away the body and buried it and went and told Jesus. When Jesus heard it, He departed from there by boat to a deserted place by Himself. But when the multitudes heard it, they followed Him on foot from the cities. And when Jesus went out, He saw a great multitude; and He was moved with compassion for them and healed their sick.

When it was evening, His disciples came to Him, saying, "This is a deserted place, and the hour is already late. Send the multitudes away, that they may go into the villages and buy themselves food."

But Jesus said to them, "They do not need to go away. You give them something to eat."

And they said to Him, "We have here only five loaves and two fish."

He said, "Bring them here to Me." Then He commanded the multitudes to sit down on the grass. And He took the five loaves and the two fish, and looking up to heaven, He blessed and broke and gave the loaves to the disciples; and the disciples gave to the multitudes. So, they all ate and were filled, and they took up twelve baskets full of the fragments that remained. Now, those who had eaten were about five thousand men, besides women and children.

Immediately, Jesus made His disciples get into the boat and go before Him to the other side, while He sent the multitudes away. And when He had sent the multitudes away, He went up on the mountain by Himself to pray.

Now, when evening came, He was alone there. But the boat was now in the middle of the sea, tossed by the waves, for the wind was contrary. Now, in the fourth watch of the night, Jesus went to them, walking on the sea. And when the disciples saw Him walking on the sea, they were troubled, saying, "It is a ghost!" And they cried out for fear.

But immediately Jesus spoke to them, saying, "Be of good cheer! It is I; do not be afraid."

And Peter answered Him and said, "Lord, if it is You, command me to come to You on the water."

So, He said, "Come." And when Peter had come down out of the boat, he walked on the water to go to Jesus.

But when he saw that the wind was boisterous, he was afraid; and beginning to sink he cried out, saying, "Lord, save me!"

And immediately Jesus stretched out His hand and caught him, and said to him, "O, you of little faith, why did you doubt?" **And when they got into the boat, the wind ceased. Then those who were in the boat came and worshipped Him, saying, "Truly, You are the Son of God."'**

Matthew 14: 6–33; 15: 32–38 NKJV

Matthew 18: 1–7

'At that time, the disciples came to Jesus, saying, "Who then is greatest in the kingdom of heaven?"

Then Jesus called a little child to Him, set him in the midst of them, and said, "Assuredly, I say to you, unless you are converted and become as little children, you will by no means enter the kingdom of heaven. Therefore, whoever humbles himself as this little child is the greatest in the kingdom of heaven. Whoever receives one little child like this in My name receives Me. Whoever causes one of these little ones who believe in Me to sin, it would be better for him if a millstone were hung around his neck, and he were drowned in the depth of the sea. Woe to the world because of offenses! For offenses must come, but woe to that man by whom the offense comes!"' Matthew 18: 1–7 NKJV

Matthew 26: 6–13

(In Bethany, Jesus Defends the Giving Heart)

'And when Jesus was in Bethany at the house of Simon, the leper, a woman came to Him having an alabaster flask of very costly fragrant oil, and she poured it on His head as He sat at the table. But when His disciples saw it, they were indignant, saying, "Why this waste? For this fragrant oil might have been sold for much and given to the poor."

But when Jesus was aware of it, He said to them, "Why do you trouble the woman? For she has done a good work for Me. For you have the poor with you always, but Me you do not have always.

"For in pouring this fragrant oil on My body, she did it for My burial. Assuredly, I say to you, wherever this gospel is preached in the whole world, what this woman has done will also be told as a memorial to her."

Matthew 26: 6–13 NKJV

Matthew 21: 1–11; 23: 37–39; Matthew 24: 3–44

(Jesus Returns to Jerusalem and Gives His Olivet Discourse)

'Now, when they drew near Jerusalem, and came to Bethphage, at the Mount of Olives, then Jesus sent two disciples, saying to them, "Go into the village opposite you, and immediately you will find a donkey tied, and a colt with her. Loose them and bring them to Me. And if anyone says anything to you, you shall say, 'The Lord has need of them,' and immediately he will send them." All this was done that it might be fulfilled which was spoken by the prophet, saying, "Tell the daughter of Zion, 'Behold, your King is coming to you, Lowly, and sitting on a donkey, A colt, the foal of a donkey'." So, the disciples went and did as Jesus commanded them. They brought the donkey and the colt, laid their clothes on them, and set Him on them. And a very great multitude spread their clothes on the road; others cut down branches from the trees and spread them on the road.

Then the multitudes who went before and those who followed cried out, saying, "Hosanna to the Son of David! 'Blessed is He who comes in the name of the LORD!' Hosanna in the highest!"

And when He had come into Jerusalem, all the city was moved, saying, "Who is this?"

So, the multitudes said, "This is Jesus, the prophet from Nazareth of Galilee.'"

Matthew 21: 1–11 NKJV

"O Jerusalem, Jerusalem, the one who kills the prophets and stones those who are sent to her! How often I wanted to gather your children together, as a hen gathers her chicks under her wings, but you were not willing! See! Your house is left to you desolate; for I say to you, you shall see Me no more till you say, 'Blessed is He who comes in the name of the LORD!'"

Matthew 23: 37–39 NKJV

The Olivet Discourse:

Now, as He sat on the Mount of Olives, the disciples came to Him privately, saying, "Tell us, when will these things be? And what will be the sign of Your coming, and of the end of the age?"

And Jesus answered and said to them, "Take heed that no one deceives you. For many will come in My name, saying, 'I am the Christ,' and will deceive many. And you will hear of wars and rumors of wars. See that you are not troubled; for all these things must come to pass, but the end is not yet. For nation will rise against nation, and kingdom against kingdom. And there will be famines, pestilences, and earthquakes in various places. All these are the beginning of sorrows. Then they will deliver you up to tribulation and kill you, and you will be hated by all nations for My name's sake. And then many will be offended, will betray one another, and will hate one another. Then many false prophets will rise up and deceive many. And because lawlessness will abound, the love of many will grow cold. But he who endures to the end, shall be saved. And this gospel of the kingdom will be preached in all the world as a witness to all the nations, and then the end will come.

Therefore, when you see the 'abomination of desolation,' spoken of by Daniel the prophet, standing in the holy place (whoever reads, let him understand), then let those who are in Judea flee to the mountains. Let him who is on the housetop not go down to take anything out of his house. And let him who is in the field not go back to get his clothes. But woe to those who are pregnant and to those who are nursing babies in those days! And pray that your flight may not be in winter or on the Sabbath.

For then, there will be great tribulation, such as has not been since the beginning of the world until this time, no, nor ever shall be. And unless those days were shortened, no flesh would be saved; but for the elect's sake those days will be shortened. Then if anyone says to you, 'Look, here is the Christ!' or 'There!' do not believe it. For false Christs and false prophets will rise and show great signs and wonders to deceive, if possible, even the elect. See, I have told you beforehand. Therefore, if they say to you, 'Look, He is in the desert!' do not go out; or 'Look, He is in the inner rooms!' do not believe it. For as the lightning comes from the east and flashes to the west, so also will the coming of the Son of Man be. For wherever the carcass is, there the eagles will be gathered together.

Immediately, after the tribulation of those days, the sun will be darkened, and the moon will not give its light; the stars will fall from heaven, and the powers of the heavens will be shaken. Then the sign of the Son of Man will appear in heaven, and then all the tribes of the earth will mourn, and they will see the Son of Man coming on the clouds of heaven with power and great glory. And He will send His angels with a great sound of a trumpet, and they will gather together His elect from the four winds, from one end of heaven to the other.

Now, learn this parable from the fig tree: When its branch has already become tender and puts forth leaves, you know that summer is near. So, you also, when you see all these things, know that it is near—at the doors! Assuredly, I say to you, this generation will by no means pass away till all these things take place. Heaven and earth will pass away, but My words will by no means pass away. 'But of that day and hour no one knows, not even the angels of heaven, but My Father only. But as the days of Noah were, so also will the coming of the Son of Man be. For as in the days before the flood, they were eating and drinking, marrying and giving in marriage, until the day that Noah entered the ark, and did not know until the flood came and took them all away, so also will the coming of the Son of Man be. Then two men will be in the field: one will be taken and the other left. Two women will be grinding at the mill: one will be taken and the other left. Watch therefore, for you do not know what hour your Lord is coming. But know this, that if the master of the house had known what hour the thief would come, he would have watched and not allowed his house to be broken into. Therefore, you also be ready, for the Son of Man is coming at an hour you do not expect.'"

Matthew 24: 3–44 NKJV

Matthew 27: 1–2, 11–14, 27–31, 39–44, 50–54 NKJV

'When morning came, all the chief priests and elders of the people plotted against Jesus to put Him to death. And when they had bound Him, they led Him away and delivered Him to Pontius Pilate the governor.'

Matthew 27: 1–2

Now Jesus stood before the governor. And the governor asked Him, saying, "Are You the King of the Jews?"

Jesus said to him, " It is as you say." And while He was being accused by the chief priests and elders, He answered nothing.

Then Pilate said to Him, "Do You not hear how many things they testify against You?" But He answered him not one word, so that the governor marveled greatly.'

Matthew 27: 11–14

'Then the soldiers of the governor took Jesus into the Praetorium and gathered the whole garrison around Him. And they stripped Him and put a scarlet robe on Him. When they had twisted a crown of thorns, they put it on His head, and a reed in His right hand. And they bowed the knee before Him and mocked Him, saying, "Hail, King of the Jews!" Then they spat on Him and took the reed and struck Him on the head. And when they had mocked Him, they took the robe off Him, put His own clothes on Him, and led Him away to be crucified.'

Matthew 27: 27–31 NKJV

'And those who passed by blasphemed Him, wagging their heads and saying, "You who destroy the temple and build it in three days, save Yourself! If You are the Son of God, come down from the cross."

Likewise, the chief priests also, mocking with the scribes and elders, said, "He saved others; Himself He cannot save. If He is the King of Israel, let Him now come down from the cross, and we will believe Him. He trusted in God; let Him deliver Him now if He will have Him; for He said, 'I am the Son of

God'." Even the robbers who were crucified with Him reviled Him with the same thing.'

Matthew 27: 39–44 NKJV

'And Jesus cried out again with a loud voice and yielded up His spirit. Then, behold, the veil of the temple was torn in two from top to bottom; and the earth quaked, and the rocks were split, and the graves were opened; and many bodies of the saints who had fallen asleep were raised; and coming out of the graves after His resurrection, they went into the holy city and appeared to many. So, when the centurion and those with him, who were guarding Jesus, saw the earthquake and the things that had happened, they feared greatly, saying, "Truly this was the Son of God!"'

Matthew 27: 50–54 NKJV

Appendix D
The Gospel of John (John 1–21)

'In the beginning was the Word, and the Word was with God, and the Word was God. He was in the beginning with God. All things were made through Him, and without Him nothing was made that was made. In Him was life, and the life was the light of men. And the light shines in the darkness, and the darkness did not comprehend it.

And the Word became flesh and dwelled among us, and we beheld His glory, the glory as of the only begotten of the Father, full of grace and truth. And of His fullness we have all received, and grace for grace.

For the law was given through Moses, but grace and truth came through Jesus Christ. No one has seen God at any time. The only begotten Son, who is in the bosom of the Father, He has declared Him.'

John 1: 1–5, 14, 16–18; NKJV

'For God so loved the world that He gave His only begotten Son, that whoever believes in Him should not perish but have everlasting life. For God did not send His Son into the world to condemn the world, but that the world through Him might be saved. 'He who believes in Him is not condemned; but he who does not believe is condemned already, because he has not believed in the name of the only begotten Son of God. And this is the condemnation, that the light has come into the world, and men loved darkness rather than light, because their deeds were evil. For everyone practicing evil hates the light and does not come to the light, lest his deeds should be exposed. But he who does the truth comes to the light, that his deeds may be clearly seen, that they have been done in God'.'

John 3: 16–21 NKJV

'Jesus answered them and said, "Most assuredly, I say to you, you seek Me, not because you saw the signs, but because you ate of the loaves and were filled. Do not labor for the food which perishes, but for the food which endures to everlasting life, which the Son of Man will give you, because God the Father has set His seal on Him.”

Then they said to Him, “What shall we do, that we may work the works of God?”

Jesus answered and said to them, “This is the work of God, that you believe in Him whom He sent.”

Therefore, they said to Him, “What sign will You perform then, that we may see it and believe You? What work will You do? Our fathers ate the manna in the desert; as it is written, ‘He gave them bread from heaven to eat’.”

Then Jesus said to them, “Most assuredly, I say to you, Moses did not give you the bread from heaven, but My Father gives you the true bread from heaven. For the bread of God is He who comes down from heaven and gives life to the world.”

Then they said to Him, “Lord, give us this bread always.”

And Jesus said to them, “I am the bread of life. He who comes to Me shall never hunger, and he who believes in Me shall never thirst. But I said to you that you have seen Me and yet do not believe. All that the Father gives Me will come to Me, and the one who comes to Me I will by no means cast out. For I have come down from heaven, not to do My own will, but the will of Him who sent Me.

This is the will of the Father who sent Me, that of all He has given Me I should lose nothing but should raise it up at the last day. And this is the will of Him who sent Me, that everyone who sees the Son and believes in Him may have everlasting life; and I will raise him up at the last day.”’

John 6: 26–40 NKJV

‘On the last day, that great day of the feast, Jesus stood and cried out, saying, “If anyone thirsts, let him come to Me and drink. He who believes in Me, as the Scripture has said, out of his heart will flow rivers of living water.” But this, He spoke concerning the Spirit, whom those believing in Him would receive; for the Holy Spirit was not yet given, because Jesus was not yet glorified.’

John 7: 37–39 NKJV

'Then Jesus spoke to them again, saying, "I am the light of the world. He who follows Me shall not walk in darkness but have the light of life."'

John 8: 12 NKJV

"Now my soul is deeply troubled. Should I pray, 'Father, save me from this hour'? But this is the very reason I came! Father, bring glory to your name."

Then a voice spoke from heaven, saying, "I have already brought glory to my name, and I will do so again." When the crowd heard the voice, some thought it was thunder, while others declared an angel had spoken to him. Then

Jesus told them, "The voice was for your benefit, not mine. The time for judging this world has come, when Satan, the ruler of this world, will be cast out. **And when I am lifted up from the earth, I will draw everyone to myself.**" He said this to indicate how he was going to die.

The crowd responded, "We understood from Scripture that the Messiah would live forever. How can you say the Son of Man will die? Just who is this Son of Man, anyway?"

Jesus replied, "My light will shine for you just a little longer. Walk in the light while you can, so the darkness will not overtake you. Those who walk in the darkness cannot see where they are going. Put your trust in the light while there is still time; then you will become children of the light." After saying these things, Jesus went away and was hidden from them.'

John 12: 27–36 NLT

'Now before the Feast of the Passover, when Jesus knew that His hour had come that He should depart from this world to the Father, having loved His own who were in the world, He loved them to the end. And supper being ended, the devil having already put it into the heart of Judas Iscariot, Simon's son, to betray Him, Jesus, knowing that the Father had given all things into His hands, and that He had come from God and was going to God, rose from supper and laid aside His garments, took a towel and girded Himself. After that, He poured water into a basin and began to wash the disciples' feet, and to wipe them with the towel with which He was girded. Then He came to Simon Peter. And Peter said to Him, "Lord, are You washing my feet?"

Jesus answered and said to him, "What I am doing you do not understand now, but you will know after this."'

John 13: 1–7 NKJV

"A little while longer and the world will see Me no more, but you will see Me. Because I live, you will live also. At that day, you will know that I am in My Father, and you in Me, and I in you. He who has My commandments and keeps them, it is he who loves Me. And he who loves Me will be loved by My Father, and I will love him and manifest Myself to him."

Jesus answered and said to him, "If anyone loves Me, he will keep My word; and My Father will love him, and We will come to him and make Our home with him."

John 14: 19–21, 23 NKJV

'I am the true vine, and My Father is the vinedresser. Every branch in Me that does not bear fruit He takes away; and every branch that bears fruit He prunes, that it may bear more fruit. You are already clean because of the word which I have spoken to you. Abide in Me, and I in you. As the branch cannot bear fruit of itself, unless it abides in the vine, neither can you, unless you abide in Me. I am the vine, you are the branches. He who abides in Me, and I in him, bears much fruit; for without Me you can do nothing. If anyone does not abide in Me, he is cast out as a branch and is withered; and they gather them and throw them into the fire, and they are burned. If you abide in Me, and My words abide in you, you will ask what you desire, and it shall be done for you. By this My Father is glorified, that you bear much fruit; so, you will be My disciples.'

John 15: 1–8 NKJV

'As the Father loved Me, I also have loved you; abide in My love. If you keep My commandments, you will abide in My love, just as I have kept My Father's commandments and abide in His love. "These things I have spoken to you, that My joy may remain in you, and that your joy may be full. This is My commandment, that you love one another as I have loved you. Greater love has no one than this, than to lay down one's life for his friends. You are My friends if you do whatever I command you. No longer do I call you servants, for a servant does not know what his master is doing; but I have called you friends, for all things that I heard from My Father I have made known to you. You did not choose Me, but I chose you and appointed you that you should go and bear fruit, and that your fruit should remain, that whatever you ask the Father in My name He may give you. These things I command you, that you love one another."'

John 15: 9–17 NKJV

'I still have many things to say to you, but you cannot bear them now. However, when He, the Spirit of truth, has come, He will guide you into all truth; for He will not speak on His own authority, but whatever He hears, He will speak; and He will tell you things to come. He will glorify Me, for He will take of what is Mine and declare it to you. All things that the Father has are Mine. Therefore, I said that He will take of Mine and declare it to you.'

John 16: 12–15 NKJV

'Now Jesus knew that they desired to ask Him, and He said to them, "Are you inquiring among yourselves about what I said, 'A little while, and you will not see Me; and again, a little while, and you will see Me?' Most assuredly, I say to you that you will weep and lament, but the world will rejoice; and you will be sorrowful, but your sorrow will be turned into joy. A woman, when she is in labor, has sorrow because her hour has come; but as soon as she has given birth to the child, she no longer remembers the anguish, for joy that a human being has been born into the world. Therefore, you now have sorrow; but I will see you again and your heart will rejoice, and your joy no one will take from you. And in that day you will ask Me nothing. Most assuredly, I say to you, whatever you ask the Father in My name He will give you. Until now you have asked nothing in My name. Ask, and you will receive, that your joy may be full."'

John 16: 19–24 NKJV

'Indeed, the hour is coming, yes, has now come, that you will be scattered, each to his own, and will leave Me alone. And yet I am not alone, because the Father is with Me. These things I have spoken to you, that in Me you may have peace. In the world you will have tribulation; but be of good cheer, I have overcome the world.'

John 16: 32–33 NKJV

Jesus Prays in the Garden

'After saying all these things, Jesus looked up to heaven and said, "Father, the hour has come. Glorify your Son, so he can give glory back to you. For you have given him authority over everyone. He gives eternal life to each one you have given him. And this is the way to have eternal life—to know you, the only true God, and Jesus Christ, the one you sent to earth. I brought glory to you here on earth by completing the work you gave me to do. Now, Father, bring me into the glory we shared before the world began."'

(John 17: 1–5 NLT)

'I have manifested Your name to the men whom You have given Me out of the world. They were Yours, You gave them to Me, and they have kept Your word. Now they have known that all things which You have given Me are from You. For I have given to them the words which You have given Me; and they have received them and have known surely that I came forth from You; and they have believed that You sent Me. I pray for them. I do not pray for the world but for those whom You have given Me, for they are Yours. And all Mine are Yours, and Yours are Mine, and I am glorified in them. Now I am no longer in the world, but these are in the world, and I come to You. Holy Father, keep through Your name those whom You have given Me, that they may be one as We are. While I was with them in the world, I kept them in Your name. Those whom You gave Me I have kept; and none of them is lost except the son of perdition, that the Scripture might be fulfilled. But now, I come to You, and these things I speak in the world, that they may have My joy fulfilled in themselves. I have given them Your word; and the world has hated them because they are not of the world, just as I am not of the world. I do not pray that You should take them out of the world, but that You should keep them from the evil one. Sanctify them by Your truth. Your word is truth. As You sent Me into the world, I also have sent them into the world. And for their sakes I sanctify Myself, that they also may be sanctified by the truth.'

John 17: 6–15, 17–19 NKJV (Jesus Prays for His Disciples)

'I do not pray for these alone, but also for those who will believe in Me through their word; that they all may be one, as You, Father, are in Me, and I in You; that they also may be one in Us, that the world may believe that You sent Me. And the glory which You gave Me I have given them, that they may be one just as We are one: I in them, and You in Me; that they may be made perfect in one, and that the world may know that You have sent Me, and have loved them as You have loved Me. Father, I desire that they also whom You gave Me may be with Me where I am, that they may behold My glory which You have given Me; for You loved Me before the foundation of the world. O righteous Father! The world has not known You, but I have known You; and these have known that You sent Me. And I have declared to them Your name, and will declare it, that the love with which You loved Me may be in them, and I in them.'

John 17: 20–26 NKJV (Jesus Prays for All Believers)

'After saying these things, Jesus crossed the Kidron Valley with his disciples and entered a grove of olive trees. Judas, the betrayer, knew this place, because Jesus had often gone there with his disciples.

The leading priests and Pharisees had given Judas a contingent of Roman soldiers and temple guards to accompany him. Now, with blazing torches, lanterns, and weapons, they arrived at the olive grove. Jesus fully realized all that was going to happen to him, so he stepped forward to meet them. "Who are you looking for?" He asked.

"Jesus, the Nazarene," they replied.

"I Am he," Jesus said. (Judas, who betrayed him, was standing with them.) As Jesus said, "I Am he," they all drew back and fell to the ground!

Once more he asked them, "Who are you looking for?"

And again, they replied, "Jesus the Nazarene."

"I told you that I Am he," Jesus said. "And since I am the one you want, let these others go."

He did this to fulfill his own statement: 'I did not lose a single one of those you have given me.' Then, Simon Peter drew a sword and slashed off the right ear of Malchus, the high priest's slave. But Jesus said to Peter, "Put your sword back into its sheath. **Shall I not drink from the cup of suffering the Father has given me"?'**

John 18: 1–11 NLT

'Then the servant girl who kept the door said to Peter, "You are not also one of this Man's disciples, are you?"

He said, "I am not." Now. Simon Peter stood and warmed himself.

Therefore, they said to him, "You are not also one of His disciples, are you?"

He denied it and said, "I am not!"

One of the servants of the high priest, a relative of him whose ear Peter cut off, said, "Did I not see you in the garden with Him?" Peter then denied again; and immediately a rooster crowed.'

John 18: 17, 25–27 NKJV

'And He, bearing His cross, went out to a place called the Place of a Skull, which is called in Hebrew, Golgotha, where they crucified Him, and two others with Him, one on either side, and Jesus in the center. Now, Pilate wrote a title and put it on the cross. And the writing was: JESUS OF NAZARETH, THE KING OF THE JEWS. Then many of the Jews read this title, for the place where Jesus was crucified was near the city; and it was written in Hebrew, Greek, and Latin. Therefore, the chief priests of the Jews said to Pilate, "Do not write, 'The King of the Jews,' but He said, 'I am the King of the Jews.'"

Pilate answered, "What I have written, I have written." Then the soldiers, when they had crucified Jesus, took His garments and made four parts, to each soldier a part, and also the tunic. Now the tunic was without seam, woven from the top in one piece.

They said therefore among themselves, "Let us not tear it, but cast lots for it, whose it shall be," that the Scripture might be fulfilled which says: 'They divided My garments among them, And for My clothing they cast lots.' Therefore, the soldiers did these things. Now, there stood by the cross of Jesus His mother, and His mother's sister, Mary the wife of Clopas, and Mary Magdalene. When Jesus therefore saw His mother, and the disciple whom He loved standing by, He said to His mother, "Woman, behold your son!"

Then He said to the disciple, "Behold your mother!" And from that hour, that disciple took her to his own home. After this, Jesus, knowing that all things were now accomplished, that the Scripture might be fulfilled, said, "I thirst!" Now a vessel full of sour wine was sitting there; and they filled a sponge with sour wine, put it on hyssop, and put it to His mouth. So, when Jesus had received the sour wine, He said, "It is finished!" And bowing His head, He gave up His spirit.'

John 19: 17–30 NKJV

'Now, on the first day of the week, Mary Magdalene went to the tomb early, while it was still dark, and saw that the stone had been taken away from the tomb. Then she ran and came to Simon Peter, and to the other disciple, whom Jesus loved, and said to them, "They have taken away the Lord out of the tomb, and we do not know where they have laid Him." Peter therefore went out, and the other disciple, and were going to the tomb. So, they both ran together, and the other disciple outran Peter and came to the tomb first. And he, stooping down and looking in, saw the linen cloths lying there; yet he did not go in. Then Simon Peter came, following him, and went into the tomb; and he saw the linen cloths lying there, and the handkerchief that had been around His head, not lying with the linen cloths, but folded together in a place by itself.

Then the other disciple, who came to the tomb first, went in also; and he saw and believed. For as yet they did not know the Scripture, that He must rise again from the dead. Then the disciples went away again to their own homes.

But Mary stood outside by the tomb weeping, and as she wept, she stooped down and looked into the tomb. And she saw two angels in white sitting, one at the head and the other at the feet, where the body of Jesus had lain. Then they said to her, "Woman, why are you weeping?"

She said to them, "Because they have taken away my Lord, and I do not know where they have laid Him." Now, when she had said this, she turned around and saw Jesus standing there, and did not know that it was Jesus.

Jesus said to her, "Woman, why are you weeping? Whom are you seeking?"

She, supposing Him to be the gardener, said to Him, "Sir, if You have carried Him away, tell me where You have laid Him, and I will take Him away."

Jesus said to her, "Mary!" S

he turned and said to Him, "Rabboni!" (which is to say, Teacher).

Jesus said to her, "Do not cling to Me, for I have not yet ascended to My Father; but go to My brethren and say to them, 'I am ascending to My Father and your Father, and to My God and your God'." Mary Magdalene came and told the disciples that she had seen the Lord, and that He had spoken these things to her.

Then, the same day at evening, being the first day of the week, when the doors were shut where the disciples were assembled, for fear of the Jews, Jesus came and stood in the midst, and said to them, "Peace be with you." When He had said this, He showed them His hands and His side. Then the disciples were glad when they saw the Lord. So, Jesus said to them again, "Peace to you! As the Father has sent Me, I also send you." And when He had said this, He breathed on them, and said to them, "Receive the Holy Spirit. If you forgive the sins of any, they are forgiven them; if you retain the sins of any, they are retained."'

John 20: 1–23 NKJV

'Now Thomas, called the Twin, one of the twelve, was not with them when Jesus came. The other disciples therefore said to him, "We have seen the Lord."

So, he said to them, "Unless I see in His hands the print of the nails and put my finger into the print of the nails, and put my hand into His side, I will not believe."' John 20: 24–25 NKJV

'So, when they had eaten breakfast, Jesus said to Simon Peter, "Simon, son of Jonah, do you love Me more than these?"

He said to Him, "Yes, Lord; You know that I love You."

He said to him, "Feed My lambs."

He said to him again a second time, "Simon, son of Jonah, do you love Me?"

He said to Him, "Yes, Lord; You know that I love You."

He said to him, "Tend My sheep."

He said to him the third time, "Simon, son of Jonah, do you love Me?"

Peter was grieved because He said to him the third time, "Do you love Me?"

And he said to Him, "Lord, You know all things; You know that I love You."

Jesus said to him, "Feed My sheep."'

John 21: 15–17 NKJV

Appendix E
The First Epistle of John (1 John 1–5)

1 JOHN 1: 5–7; 2: 29)
(GOD IS LIGHT)

'This is the message which we have heard from Him and declare to you, that God is light and in Him is no darkness at all. If we say that we have fellowship with Him, and walk in darkness, we lie and do not practice the truth. But if we walk in the light as He is in the light, we have fellowship with one another, and the blood of Jesus Christ His Son cleanses us from all sin.' (*Emphasis added*)

I John 1: 5–7 NKJV

'If you know that He is righteous, you know that everyone who practices righteousness is born of Him.'

I John 2: 29 NKJV

1 JOHN 3–4
(GOD IS LOVE)

'Behold what manner of love the Father has bestowed on us, that we should be called children of God! Therefore, the world does not know us, because it did not know Him. Beloved, now we are children of God; and it has not yet been revealed what we shall be, but we know that when He is revealed, we shall be like Him, for we shall see Him as He is. And everyone who has this hope in Him purifies himself, just as He is pure. By this we know love, because He laid down His life for us. And we also ought to lay down our lives for the brethren. But whoever has this world's goods, and sees his brother in need, and shuts up his heart from him, how does the love of God abide in him? My little children, let us not love in word or in tongue, but in deed, and in truth. And by this we know that we are of the truth and shall assure our hearts before Him.

For if our heart condemns us, God is greater than our heart, and knows all things. Beloved, if our heart does not condemn us, we have confidence toward God. Now, he who keeps His commandments abides in Him, and He in him. And by this we know that He abides in us, by the Spirit whom He has given us.'

I John 3: 1–3, 16–21, 24 NKJV

'By this you know the Spirit of God: Every spirit that confesses that Jesus Christ has come in the flesh is of God, and every spirit that does not confess that Jesus Christ has come in the flesh is not of God. And this is the spirit of the Antichrist, which you have heard was coming, and is now already in the world.'

1 John 4: 2–3

You are of God, little children, and have overcome them, because He who is in you is greater than he who is in the world. They are of the world. Therefore, they speak as of the world, and the world hears them. We are of God. He who knows God hears us; he who is not of God does not hear us. By this we know the spirit of truth and the spirit of error.

1 John 4: 4–6

'Beloved, let us love one another, for love is of God; and everyone who loves is born of God and knows God. He who does not love does not know God, for God is love. In this the love of God was manifested toward us, that God has sent His only begotten Son into the world, that we might live through Him. In this is love, not that we loved God, but that He loved us and sent His Son to be the propitiation for our sins. Beloved, if God so loved us, we also ought to love one another.'

I John 4: 7–11 NKJV

No one has seen God at any time. If we love one another, God abides in us, and His love has been perfected in us. By this, we know that we abide in Him, and He in us, because He has given us of His Spirit. And we have seen and testify that the Father has sent the Son as Savior of the world. Whoever confesses that Jesus is the Son of God, God abides in him, and he in God. And we have known and believed the love that God has for us. ***God is love, and he who abides in love abides in God, and God in him.*** I John 4: 14–16 NKJV

Love has been perfected among us in this: that we may have boldness in the day of judgment; because as He is, so are we in this world. There is no fear in love; but perfect love casts out fear, because fear involves torment. But he who fears has not been made perfect in love. We love Him because He first loved us. If someone says, "I love God," and hates his brother, he is a liar; for he who does not love his brother whom he has seen, how can he love God whom he has not seen? And this commandment we have from Him: that he who loves God must love his brother also.

I John 4: 17–21 NKJV

1 JOHN 5: 1–15, 20
(GOD IS LIFE)

'Whoever believes that Jesus is the Christ is born of God, and everyone who loves Him who begot also loves him who is begotten of Him. By this we know that we love the children of God, when we love God and keep His commandments. For this is the love of God, that we keep His commandments. And His commandments are not burdensome. For whatever is born of God overcomes the world. And this is the victory that has overcome the world— our faith. Who is he who overcomes the world, but he who believes that Jesus is the Son of God? This is He who came by water and blood—Jesus Christ; not only by water, but by water and blood. And it is the Spirit who bears witness, because the Spirit is truth. For there are three that bear witness in heaven: the Father, the Word, and the Holy Spirit; and these three are one. And there are three that bear witness on earth: the Spirit, the water, and the blood; and these three agree as one. If we receive the witness of men, the witness of God is greater; for this is the witness of God which He has testified of His Son. He who believes in the Son of God has the witness in himself; he who does not believe God has made Him a liar, because he has not believed the testimony that God has given of His Son. **And this is the testimony: that God has given us eternal life, and this life is in His Son. He who has the Son has life; he who does not have the Son of God does not have life**. These things I have written to you who believe in the name of the Son of God, that you may know that you have eternal life, and that you may continue to believe in the name of the Son of God. Now, this is the confidence that we have in Him, that if we ask anything according to His will, He hears us. And if we know that He hears us, whatever we ask, we know that we have the petitions that we have asked of Him. And we know that the Son of God has come and has given us an understanding, that we may know Him who is true; and we are in Him who is true, in His Son Jesus Christ. This is the true God and eternal life.'

I John 5: 1–15, 20 NKJV

Appendix F
Revelation (Revelation 1–22)

The Whole Story of Redemption and Salvation

'The Revelation of Jesus Christ, which God gave Him to show His servants—things which must shortly take place. And He sent and signified it by His angel to His servant John, who bore witness to the word of God, and to the testimony of Jesus Christ, to all things that he saw. **Blessed is he who reads and those who hear the words of this prophecy and keep those things which are written in it; for the time is near.'**

Revelation 1: 1–3 NKJV

'John, to the seven churches which are in Asia: Grace to you and peace from Him who is and who was and who is to come, and from the seven Spirits who are before His throne, and from Jesus Christ, the faithful witness, the firstborn from the dead, and the ruler over the kings of the earth. To Him who loved us and washed us from our sins in His own blood and has made us kings and priests to His God and Father, to Him be glory and dominion forever and ever. Amen. Behold, He is coming with clouds, and every eye will see Him, even they who pierced Him. And all the tribes of the earth will mourn because of Him. Even so, Amen.'

Revelation 1: 4–7 NKJV

"I am the Alpha and the Omega, the Beginning and the End," says the Lord, "who is and who was and who is to come, the Almighty."

Revelation 1: 8 NKJV

'I was in the Spirit on the Lord's Day, and I heard behind me a loud voice, as of a trumpet, saying, "I am the Alpha and the Omega, the First and the Last," and, "What you see, write in a book and send it to the seven churches which are in Asia: to Ephesus, to Smyrna, to Pergamos, to Thyatira, to Sardis, to Philadelphia, and to Laodicea." Then I turned to see the voice that spoke with me. And having turned I saw seven golden lampstands, and in the midst of the seven lampstands One like the Son of Man, clothed with a garment down to the feet and girded about the chest with a golden band. His head and hair were white like wool, as white as snow, and His eyes like a flame of fire; His feet were like fine brass, as if refined in a furnace, and His voice as the sound of many waters; He had in His right hand seven stars, out of His mouth went a sharp two-edged sword, and His countenance was like the sun shining in its strength. And when I saw Him, I fell at His feet as dead. But He laid His right hand on me, saying to me, "Do not be afraid; I am the First and the Last. I am He who lives, and was dead, and behold, I am alive forevermore. Amen. And I have the keys of Hades and of Death. Write the things which you have seen, and the things which are, and the things which will take place after this. The mystery of the seven stars which you saw in My right hand, and the seven golden lampstands: The seven stars are the angels of the seven churches, and the seven lampstands which you saw are the seven churches.'"

Revelation 1: 10–20 NKJV

The Loveless Church

To the angel of the Church of Ephesus write, 'These things says He who holds the seven stars in His right hand, who walks in the midst of the seven golden lampstands: "I know your works, your labor, your patience, and that you cannot bear those who are evil. And you have tested those who say they are Apostles and are not and have found them liars; and you have persevered and have patience and have labored for My name's sake and have not become weary. Nevertheless, I have this against you, that you have left your first love. He who has an ear, let him hear what the Spirit says to the churches. **To him who overcomes I will give to eat from the tree of life, which is in the midst of the Paradise of God.'"**

Revelation 2: 1–4, 7 NKJV

The Persecuted Church

And to the angel of the Church in Smyrna write, 'These things says the First and the Last, who was dead, and came to life: "I know your works, tribulation, and poverty (but you are rich); and I know the blasphemy of those

who say they are Jews and are not but are a synagogue of Satan. Do not fear any of those things which you are about to suffer. Indeed, the devil is about to throw some of you into prison, that you may be tested, and you will have tribulation ten days. **Be faithful until death, and I will give you the crown of life. He who has an ear, let him hear what the Spirit says to the churches. He who overcomes shall not be hurt by the second death.'"**
Revelation 2: 8–11 NKJV

The Compromising Church

And to the angel of the Church in Pergamos write, 'These things says He who has the sharp two-edged sword: "I know your works, and where you dwell, where Satan's throne is. And you hold fast to My name and did not deny My faith even in the days in which Antipas was My faithful martyr, who was killed among you, where Satan dwells. But I have a few things against you, because you have there, those who hold the doctrine of Balaam, who taught Balak to put a stumbling block before the children of Israel, to eat things sacrificed to idols, and to commit sexual immorality. Thus, you also have those who hold the doctrine of the Nicolaitans, which thing I hate. **Repent, or else I will come to you quickly and will fight against them with the sword of My mouth.'"**
Revelation 2: 12–16 NKJV

The Corrupt Church

And to the angel of the Church in Thyatira write, 'These things says the Son of God, who has eyes like a flame of fire, and His feet like fine brass: "I know your works, love, service, faith, and your patience; and as for your works, the last are more than the first. Nevertheless, I have a few things against you, because you allow that woman Jezebel, who calls herself a prophetess, to teach and seduce My servants to commit sexual immorality and eat things sacrificed to idols. And I gave her time to repent of her sexual immorality, and she did not repent. Indeed, I will cast her into a sickbed, and those who commit adultery with her into great tribulation, unless they repent of their deeds. I will kill her children with death, and all the churches shall know that I am He who searches the minds and hearts. And I will give to each one of you according to your works. Now to you I say, and to the rest in Thyatira, as many as do not have this doctrine, who have not known the depths of Satan, as they say, I will put on you no other burden. **But hold fast what you have till I come.**

And he who overcomes, and keeps My works until the end, to him I will give power over the nations—"'
Revelation 2: 18–26 NKJV

The Dead Church

And to the angel of the Church in Sardis write, 'These things says He who has the seven Spirits of God and the seven stars: "I know your works, that you have a name that you are alive, but you are dead. Be watchful, and strengthen the things which remain, that are ready to die, for I have not found your works perfect before God. Remember therefore how you have received and heard; hold fast and repent. Therefore, if you will not watch, I will come upon you as a thief, and you will not know what hour I will come upon you. You have a few names even in Sardis who have not defiled their garments; and they shall walk with Me in white, for they are worthy. **He who overcomes shall be clothed in white garments, and I will not blot out his name from the Book of Life; but I will confess his name before My Father and before His angels."'** Revelation 3: 1–5 NKJV

The Faithful Church

And to the angel of the Church in Philadelphia write, 'These things says He who is holy, He who is true, He who has the key of David, He who opens and no one shuts, and shuts and no one opens: I know your works. See, I have set before you an open door, and no one can shut it; for you have a little strength, have kept My word, and have not denied My name. Indeed, I will make those of the synagogue of Satan, who say they are Jews and are not, but lie—indeed I will make them come and worship before your feet, and to know that I have loved you. Because you have kept My command to persevere, I also will keep you from the hour of trial which shall come upon the whole world, to test those who dwell on the earth. Behold, I am coming quickly! Hold fast what you have, that no one may take your crown. **He who overcomes, I will make him a pillar in the temple of My God, and he shall go out no more.**

I will write on him the name of My God and the name of the city of My God, the New Jerusalem, which comes down out of heaven from My God. And I will write on him My new name.'

Revelation 3: 7–12 NKJV

The Lukewarm Church

And to the angel of the Church of the Laodiceans write, 'These things says the Amen, the Faithful and True Witness, the Beginning of the creation of God: "I know your works, that you are neither cold nor hot. I could wish you were cold or hot. So then, because you are lukewarm, and neither cold nor hot, I will vomit you out of My mouth. Because you say, 'I am rich, have become wealthy, and have need of nothing'—and do not know that you are wretched, miserable, poor, blind, and naked—I counsel you to buy from Me gold refined in the fire, that you may be rich; and white garments, that you may be clothed, that the shame of your nakedness may not be revealed; and anoint your eyes with eye salve, that you may see. As many as I love, I rebuke and chasten. **Therefore, be zealous and repent. Behold, I stand at the door and knock. If anyone hears My voice and opens the door, I will come in to him and dine with him, and he with Me. To him who overcomes I will grant to sit with Me on My throne, as I also overcame and sat down with My Father on His throne."'**

Revelation 3: 14–21 NKJV

'After these things, I looked, and behold, a door standing open in heaven. And the first voice which I heard was like a trumpet speaking with me, saying, "Come up here, and I will show you things which must take place after this. Immediately I was in the Spirit; and behold, a throne set in heaven, and One sat on the throne. And He who sat there was like a jasper and a sardius stone in appearance; and there was a rainbow around the throne, in appearance like an emerald."'

Revelation 4: 1–3 NKJV

'Before the throne there was a sea of glass, like crystal. And in the midst of the throne, and around the throne, were four living creatures full of eyes in front and in back. The four living creatures, each having six wings, were full of eyes around and within. And they do not rest day or night, saying, "Holy, holy, holy, Lord God Almighty, Who was and is and is to come!" Whenever the living creatures give glory and honor and thanks to Him who sits on the throne, who lives forever and ever, the twenty-four elders fall down before Him who sits on the throne and worship Him who lives forever and ever, and cast their crowns before the throne, saying: "You are worthy, O Lord, To receive glory and honor and power; For You created all things, And by Your will they exist and were created."'

Revelation 4: 6, 8–11 NKJV

'And I saw in the right hand of Him who sat on the throne a scroll written inside and on the back, sealed with seven seals. Then I saw a strong angel proclaiming with a loud voice, "Who is worthy to open the scroll and to loosen its seals?" And no one in heaven or on the earth or under the earth was able to open the scroll, or to look at it. So, I wept much, because no one was found worthy to open and read the scroll, or to look at it.

But one of the elders said to me, "Do not weep. Behold, the Lion of the tribe of Judah, the Root of David, has prevailed to open the scroll and to loosen its seven seals." Then He came and took the scroll out of the right hand of Him who sat on the throne.'

Revelation 5: 1–5, 7 NKJV

'Now when He had taken the scroll, the four living creatures and the twenty-four elders fell down before the Lamb, each having a harp, and golden bowls full of incense, which are the prayers of the saints. And they sang a new song, saying: "You are worthy to take the scroll, And to open its seals; For You were slain, And have redeemed us to God by Your blood out of every tribe and tongue and people and nation, And have made us kings and priests to our God; And we shall reign on the earth." Then I looked, and I heard the voice of many angels around the throne, the living creatures, and the elders; and the number of them was ten thousand times ten thousand, and thousands of thousands, saying with a loud voice, "Worthy is the Lamb who was slain To receive power and riches and wisdom, And strength and honor and glory and blessing"!'

Revelation 5: 8–12 NKJV

'And every creature which is in heaven and on the earth and under the earth and such as are in the sea, and all that are in them, I heard saying, "Blessing and honor and glory and power Be to Him who sits on the throne, And to the Lamb, forever and ever!" Then the four living creatures said, "Amen!" And the twenty-four elders fell down and worshipped Him who lives forever and ever.'

Revelation 5: 13–14 NKJV

'Now, I saw when the Lamb opened one of the seals; and I heard one of the four living creatures saying with a voice like thunder, "Come and see." And I looked, and behold, a white horse. He who sat on it had a bow; and a crown was given to him, and he went out conquering and to conquer.'

Revelation 6: 1–2 NKJV

'When He opened the second seal, I heard the second living creature saying, "Come and see." Another horse, fiery red, went out. And it was granted to the one who sat on it to take peace from the earth, and that people should kill one another; and there was given to him a great sword.'

Revelation 6: 3–4 NKJV

'When He opened the third seal, I heard the third living creature say, "Come and see." So, I looked, and behold, a black horse, and he who sat on it had a pair of scales in his hand.

And I heard a voice in the midst of the four living creatures saying, "A quart of wheat for a denarius, and three quarts of barley for a denarius; and do not harm the oil and the wine."'

Revelation 6: 5–6 NKJV

'When He opened the fourth seal, I heard the voice of the fourth living creature saying, "Come and see." So, I looked, and behold, a pale horse. And the name of him who sat on it was Death, and Hades followed with him. And power was given to them over a fourth of the earth, to kill with sword, with hunger, with death, and by the beasts of the earth.'

Revelation 6: 7–8 NKJV

'When He opened the fifth seal, I saw under the altar the souls of those who had been slain for the word of God and for the testimony which they held. And they cried with a loud voice, saying, "How long, O Lord, holy and true, until You judge and avenge our blood on those who dwell on the earth?" Then a white robe was given to each of them; and it was said to them that they should rest a little while longer, until both the number of their fellow servants and their brethren, who would be killed as they were, was completed.'

Revelation 6: 9–11 NKJV

'I looked when He opened the sixth seal, and behold, there was a great earthquake; and the sun became black as sackcloth of hair, and the moon became like blood. And the stars of heaven fell to the earth, as a fig tree drops its late figs when it is shaken by a mighty wind. Then the sky receded as a scroll when it is rolled up, and every mountain and island was moved out of its place. And the kings of the earth, the great men, the rich men, the commanders, the mighty men, every slave and every free man, hid themselves in the caves and in the rocks of the mountains, and said to the mountains and rocks, "Fall on us and hide us from the face of Him who sits on the throne and from the wrath of the Lamb! For the great day of His wrath has come, and who is able to stand?"'

Revelation 6: 12–17 NKJV

'Then I saw another angel ascending from the east, having the seal of the living God. And he cried with a loud voice to the four angels to whom it was granted to harm the earth and the sea, saying, "Do not harm the earth, the sea, or the trees till we have sealed the servants of our God on their foreheads." And I heard the number of those who were sealed. One hundred and forty-four thousand of all the tribes of the children of Israel were sealed:'

Revelation 7: 2–4 NKJV

'After these things, I looked, and behold, a great multitude which no one could number, of all nations, tribes, peoples, and tongues, standing before the throne and before the Lamb, clothed with white robes, with palm branches in their hands, and crying out with a loud voice, saying, "Salvation belongs to our God who sits on the throne, and to the Lamb!" All the angels stood around the throne and the elders and the four living creatures and fell on their faces before the throne and worshipped God, saying, "Amen! Blessing and glory and wisdom, Thanksgiving and honor and power and might, Be to our God forever and ever. Amen."' Revelation 7: 9–12 NKJV

'Then one of the elders answered, saying to me, **"Who are these arrayed in white robes, and where did they come from?"**

And I said to him, "Sir, you know."
So, he said to me, "These are the ones who come out of the great tribulation, and washed their robes and made them white in the blood of the Lamb. Therefore, they are before the throne of God, and serve Him day and night in His temple. And He who sits on the throne will dwell among them. They shall neither hunger anymore nor thirst anymore; the sun shall not strike them, nor any heat; for the Lamb who is in the midst

of the throne will shepherd them and lead them to living fountains of waters. And God will wipe away every tear from their eyes."'

Revelation 7: 13–17 NKJV

'When He opened the seventh seal, there was silence in heaven for about half an hour. And I saw the seven angels who stand before God, and to them were given seven trumpets. Then another angel, having a golden censer, came and stood at the altar. He was given much incense, that he should offer it with the prayers of all the saints upon the golden altar which was before the throne. And the smoke of the incense, with the prayers of the saints, ascended before God from the angel's hand. Then the angel took the censer, filled it with fire from the altar, and threw it to the earth. And there were noises, thundering, lightnings, and an earthquake. So, the seven angels who had the seven trumpets prepared themselves to sound.'

Revelation 8: 1–6 NKJV

'Then the seventh angel sounded: And there were loud voices in heaven, saying, "The kingdoms of this world have become the kingdoms of our Lord and of His Christ, and He shall reign forever and ever!"

And the twenty-four elders who sat before God on their thrones fell on their faces and worshipped God, saying: "We give You thanks, O Lord God Almighty, The One who is and who was and who is to come, Because You have taken Your great power and reigned. The nations were angry, and Your wrath has come, And the time of the dead, that they should be judged, And that You should reward Your servants the prophets and the saints, And those who fear Your name, small and great, And should destroy those who destroy the earth." Then the temple of God was opened in heaven, and the ark of His covenant was seen in His temple. And there were lightnings, noises, thundering, an earthquake, and great hail.'

Revelation 11: 15–19 NKJV

'Now a great sign appeared in heaven: a woman clothed with the sun, with the moon under her feet, and on her head a garland of twelve stars. Then being with child, she cried out in labor and in pain to give birth. And another sign appeared in heaven: behold, a great, fiery red dragon having seven heads and ten horns, and seven diadems on his heads. His tail drew a third of the stars of heaven and threw them to the earth. And the dragon stood before the woman who was ready to give birth, to devour her Child as soon as it was born. She bore a male Child who was to rule all nations with a rod of iron. And her Child was caught up to God and His throne. Then the woman fled into the wilderness, where she has a place prepared by God, that they should feed her there one thousand two hundred and sixty days. And war broke out in heaven: Michael and his angels fought with the dragon; and the dragon and his angels fought, but they did not prevail, nor was a place found for them in heaven any longer. So, the great dragon was cast out, that serpent of old, called the Devil and Satan, who deceives the whole world; he was cast to the earth, and his angels were cast out with him.

Then I heard a loud voice saying in heaven, "Now salvation, and strength, and the kingdom of our God, and the power of His Christ have come, for the accuser of our brethren, who accused them before our God day and night, has been cast down. And they overcame him by the blood of the Lamb and by the word of their testimony, and they did not love their lives to the death. Therefore, rejoice, O heavens, and you who dwell in them! Woe to the inhabitants of the earth and the sea! For the devil has come down to you, having great wrath, because he knows that he has a short time."

Now when the dragon saw that he had been cast to the earth, he persecuted the woman who gave birth to the male Child. But the woman was given two wings of a great eagle, that she might fly into the wilderness to her place, where she is nourished for a time and times and half a time, from the presence of the serpent. So, the serpent spewed water out of his mouth like a flood after the woman, that he might cause her to be carried away by the flood. But the earth helped the woman, and the earth opened its mouth and swallowed up the flood which the dragon had spewed out of his mouth. And the dragon was enraged with the woman, and he went to make war with the rest of her offspring, who keep the commandments of God and have the testimony of Jesus Christ.'

Revelation 12: 1–17 NKJV

'Here is wisdom. Let him who has understanding calculate the number of the beast, for it is the number of a man: His number is 666.'

Revelation 13: 18 NKJV

'Then I looked, and behold, a Lamb standing on Mount Zion, and with Him one hundred and forty-four thousand, having His Father's name written on their foreheads. And I heard a voice from heaven, like the voice of many waters, and like the voice of loud thunder. And I heard the sound of harpists playing their harps. They sang as it were a new song before the throne, before the four living creatures, and the elders; and no one could learn that song except the hundred and forty-four thousand who were redeemed from the earth. These are the ones who were not defiled with women, for they are virgins. These are the ones who follow the Lamb wherever He goes. These were redeemed from among men, being first fruits to God and to the Lamb. And in their mouth was found no deceit, for they are without fault before the throne of God.'

Revelation 14: 1–5 NKJV

'Then a third angel followed them, saying with a loud voice, "If anyone worships the beast and his image, and receives his mark on his forehead or on his hand, he himself shall also drink of the wine of the wrath of God, which is poured out full strength into the cup of His indignation. He shall be tormented with fire and brimstone in the presence of the holy angels and in the presence of the Lamb. And the smoke of their torment ascends forever and ever; and they have no rest day or night, who worship the beast and his image, and whoever receives the mark of his name." Here is the patience of the saints; here are those who keep the commandments of God and the faith of Jesus.

Then I heard a voice from heaven saying to me, "Write: **'Blessed are the dead who die in the Lord from now on.'"**

"Yes," says the Spirit, "that they may rest from their labors, and their works follow them."'

Revelation 14: 9–13

'Then I looked, and behold, a white cloud, and on the cloud sat One like the Son of Man, having on His head a golden crown, and in His hand a sharp sickle. And another angel came out of the temple, crying with a loud voice to Him who sat on the cloud, "Thrust in Your sickle and reap, for the time has come for You to reap, for the harvest of the earth is ripe." So, He who sat on the cloud thrust in His sickle on the earth, and the earth was reaped.'

Revelation 14: 14–16 NKJV

'And I saw something like a sea of glass mingled with fire, and those who have the victory over the beast, over his image and over his mark and over the number of his name, standing on the sea of glass, having harps of God. They sing the song of Moses, the servant of God, and the song of the Lamb, saying, "Great and marvelous are Your works, Lord God Almighty! Just and true are Your ways, O King of the saints! Who shall not fear You, O Lord, and glorify Your name? For You alone are holy. For all nations shall come and worship before You, For Your judgments have been manifested."'

Revelation 15: 2–4 NKJV

'Behold, I am coming as a thief. **Blessed is he who watches, and keeps his garments, lest he walk naked and they see his shame.**'

Revelation 16: 15 NKJV

'Then he said to me, "Write: **'Blessed are those who are called to the marriage supper of the Lamb!'"**

And he said to me, "These are the true sayings of God."'

Revelation 19: 9 NKJV

'Now, I saw heaven opened, and behold, a white horse. And He who sat on him was called Faithful and True, and in righteousness He judges and makes war. His eyes were like a flame of fire, and on His head were many crowns. He had a name written that no one knew except Himself. He was clothed with a robe dipped in blood, and His name is called the word of God. And the armies in heaven, clothed in fine linen, white and clean, followed Him on white horses. Now, out of His mouth goes a sharp sword, that with it He should strike the nations. And He Himself will rule them with a rod of iron. He Himself treads the winepress of the fierceness and wrath of Almighty God. And He has on His robe and on His thigh a name written: KING OF KINGS AND LORD OF LORDS.'

Revelation 19: 11–16 NKJV

'Then the beast was captured, and with him the false prophet who worked signs in his presence, by which he deceived those who received the mark of the beast and those who worshipped his image. These two were cast alive into the lake of fire burning with brimstone. And the rest were killed with the sword which proceeded from the mouth of Him who sat on the horse. And all the birds were filled with their flesh.'

Revelation 19: 20–21 NKJV

'And I saw thrones, and they sat on them, and judgment was committed to them. Then I saw the souls of those who had been beheaded for their witness to Jesus and for the word of God, who had not worshipped the beast or his image, and had not received his mark on their foreheads or on their hands. And they lived and reigned with Christ for a thousand years.'

Revelation 20: 4 NKJV

'Blessed and holy is he who has part in the first resurrection. Over such the second death has no power, but they shall be priests of God and

of Christ and shall reign with Him a thousand years.' Revelation 20: 6 NKJV

'Then I saw a great white throne and Him who sat on it, from whose face the earth and the heaven fled away. And there was found no place for them. And I saw the dead, small and great, standing before God, and books were opened. And another book was opened, which is the Book of Life. And the dead were judged according to their works, by the things which were written in the books. The sea gave up the dead who were in it, and Death and Hades delivered up the dead who were in them. And they were judged, each one according to his works. Then Death and Hades were cast into the lake of fire. This is the second death. And anyone not found written in the Book of Life was cast into the lake of fire.'

Revelation 20: 11–15 NKJV

'Now, I saw a new heaven and a new earth, for the first heaven and the first earth had passed away. Also, there was no more sea. Then I, John, saw the holy city, New Jerusalem, coming down out of heaven from God, prepared as a bride adorned for her husband. And I heard a loud voice from heaven saying, "Behold, the tabernacle of God is with men, and He will dwell with them, and they shall be His people. God Himself will be with them and be their God. And God will wipe away every tear from their eyes; there shall be no more death, nor sorrow, nor crying. There shall be no more pain, for the former things have passed away."

Then He who sat on the throne said, "Behold, I make all things new."

And He said to me, "Write, for these words are true and faithful."

And He said to me, "It is done! I am the Alpha and the Omega, the Beginning and the End. I will give of the fountain of the water of life freely to him who thirsts. He who overcomes shall inherit all things, and I will be his God and he shall be My son."'

Revelation 21: 1–7 NKJV

'Then one of the seven angels who had the seven bowls filled with the seven last plagues came to me and talked with me, saying, "Come, I will show you the bride, the Lamb's wife." And he carried me away in the Spirit to a great and high mountain, and showed me the great city, the holy Jerusalem, descending out of heaven from God, having the glory of God. Her light was like a most precious stone, like a jasper stone, clear as crystal.'

Revelation 21: 9–11 NKJV

'But I saw no temple in it, for the Lord God Almighty and the Lamb are its temple. The city had no need of the sun or of the moon to shine in it, for the glory of God illuminated it. The Lamb is its light. And the nations of those who are saved shall walk in its light, and the kings of the earth bring their glory and honor into it. Its gates shall not be shut at all by day (there shall be no night there). And they shall bring the glory and the honor of the nations into it. But there shall by no means enter it anything that defiles, or causes an abomination or a lie, but only those who are written in the Lamb's Book of Life.'

Revelation 21: 22–27 NKJV

'And he showed me a pure river of water of life, clear as crystal, proceeding from the throne of God and of the Lamb. In the middle of its street, and on either side of the river, was the tree of life, which bore twelve fruits, each tree yielding its fruit every month. The leaves of the tree were for the healing of the nations. And there shall be no more curse, but the throne of God and of the Lamb shall be in it, and His servants shall serve Him. They shall see His face, and His name shall be on their foreheads. There shall be no night there: They need no lamp nor light of the sun, for the Lord God gives them light. And they shall reign forever and ever.'

Revelation 22: 1–5 NKJV

'Then he said to me, "These words are faithful and true." And the Lord God of the holy prophets sent His angel to show His servants the things which must shortly take place.

"Behold, I am coming quickly! **Blessed is he who keeps the words of the prophecy of this book.**" Now, I, John, saw and heard these things. And when I heard and saw, I fell down to worship before the feet of the angel who showed me these things. Then he said to me, "See that you do not do that. For I am your fellow servant, and of your brethren the prophets, and of those who keep the words of this book. Worship God."

And he said to me, "Do not seal the words of the prophecy of this book, for the time is at hand. He who is unjust, let him be unjust still; he who is filthy, let him be filthy still; he who is righteous, let him be righteous still; he who is holy, let him be holy still."' Revelation 22: 6–11 NKJV

"And behold, I am coming quickly, and My reward is with Me, to give to every one according to his work. I am the Alpha and the Omega, the Beginning and the End, the First and the Last."

Blessed are those who do His commandments, that they may have the right to the tree of life and may enter through the gates into the city.

"I, Jesus, have sent My angel to testify to you these things in the churches. I am the Root and the Offspring of David, the Bright and Morning Star."

Revelation 22: 12–14, 16 NKJV

'And the Spirit and the bride say, "Come!"

And let him who hears say, "Come!" And let him who thirsts come. Whoever desires, let him take the water of life freely.'

Revelation 22: 17 NKJV

'For I testify to everyone who hears the words of the prophecy of this book: If anyone adds to these things, God will add to him the plagues that are written in this book; and if anyone takes away from the words of the book of this prophecy, God shall take away his part from the Book of Life, from the holy city, and from the things which are written in this book.'

Revelation 22: 18–19 NKJV

'He who testifies to these things says, "Surely I am coming quickly." Amen. Even so, come, Lord Jesus! The grace of our Lord Jesus Christ be with you all. Amen.'

Revelation 22: 20–21 NKJV

Notes

1. *YouVersion* <u>bible.com</u>: Appendices A through F.
2. Charles Spurgeon (2016) *Morning & Evening, A Devotional Classic for Daily Encouragement*, Updated New International Version, Hendrickson Publishers, Marketing, LLC, Peabody, MA 01961.
3. *Life Application Study Bible, New Living Translation,* Tyndall Charitable Trust, 1996, Tyndall House Publishers, Inc. in cooperation with Wycliffe Bible Translators, Wheaton, Illinois 60189.
4. David Guzik, <u>EnduringWord.com</u> (Commentary on the Book of Revelation).

www.ingramcontent.com/pod-product-compliance
Lightning Source LLC
Chambersburg PA
CBHW060923140726
47996CB00001B/357